Andrea Bryant

SPANIELS ROCK

For Charity

First published in Great Britain as a softback original in 2015

Typeset in Dante MT std and Emily's Candy

Design and publishing by UK Book Publishing

UK Book Publishing is a trading name of Consilience Media

www.ukbookpublishing.com

ISBN: 978-1-910223-40-6

About Us

We are passionate about our spaniels and want to raise as much money as we can for those spaniels less fortunate than ours who are still looking for their forever home.

It costs money to care for a spaniel in the many Rescue Homes before the spaniel can be re-homed. By writing this book we hope to raise some much needed funds to help support spaniels in these homes before finding their forever home.

Spaniels Rock Book has been created using real life stories from spaniels around the world. Some of the spaniels featuring in our book are rescues and have experienced the re-homing process.

We are also featuring a section in memory of some beloved spaniels that have gone over the rainbow bridge. They are truly missed by their humans and being part of this book is a tribute to their memory.

All proceeds from this book will be donated to various spaniel charities

My name is Maki and I live in Dorset, UK

I once caused a massive traffic jam on a big main road, when I decided to cross over the pedestrian crossing completely on my tummy

Name	Maki
Birthdate	09/12/2011
My Mum	Andrea
I live in	Bournemouth, Dorset, UK
My favourite toy	my furry monkey
I sleep	with my Mum on her bed, or in it when I'm too cold
Favourite treat	tuna or a slice of roast beef
Other favourite treat	raw carrot and chicken breast
Good habits	I eat a vegetable toothbrush every day for my gums
Bad habits	I steal other people's picnics when out walking. I steal my mums socks when she leaves them lying around. I present pants to the postman
Other bad habits	I have selective hearing as my mum would say when I'm out. She doesn't realise, how I just can't help myself when chasing pheasants and squirrels!
Favourite walk	Hengistbury Head, I love the variety of scents and when I get hot and bothered I can swim with the ducks.
Favourite activity	Going to visit severely disabled adults as a therapy dog.
My friends	Hedley, a Springer spaniel. I have known him since I was 12 weeks old. Hedley's family call us the Kray Twins because we do seem to get up to mischief together. Hedley's mum thought my name was Steve when she first met me and called me that on walks for some time. I still came back as I didn't want her to be embarrassed. I have lots of other doggie friends who I meet on walks.

Hi, my name is Maki. I am a three year old black and white Working Cocker Spaniel. I was born in Farnborough, Hampshire. My mum came to see me when I was 5 weeks old. Apparently I choose her as I was the only one in the litter to totter over to her and wee on her foot! She saw that as a "Sign" we were meant to be together. I haven't the heart to tell her that I actually missed the wee pad hence it landing on her foot. But that's a minor point. We are a match made in heaven. I adore my mum and I know she thinks the world of me.

Swimming with my mum

My mum calls me Captain Mak! I love going out on the boat (well more of a dingy with an electric motor) I get up close and personal with the ducks and my humans get to enjoy the scenery. This particular day, I got overly excited about being so near to the ducks. I had my life jacket on. We were sailing past loads of ducks and I think I forgot myself and decided to leap out of the boat. What was lovely, my mum joined me. She had hold of my lead and once I leaped, she leapt too! I didn't quite understand why her friends felt they had to join us as well but I think it had something to do with the boat turning upside down as I leapt out. We all bobbed around for a bit. My mum was making this funny shrieking noise which I can only describe as sheer bliss. I could tell she loved swimming with me in the river. Her paws were flapping around and she made sure she bobbed around with me. Sadly the ducks had swum off but I made sure I had a good swim around while my mum's friends dragged the boat back to the side of the river.

I love to chase squirrels, rabbits, pheasants and anything else that moves.

I love to walk around on my tummy with my back legs stretched right out. My grandma calls me Inspector Crusoe. If my mum takes me into a shop, I will enter on my belly. I also like to cross the road on my tummy, cspccially if I have an itch. I once caused a huge traffic jam when crossing over the pedestrian crossing with my mum. The lights were green for ages before we got to the other side. It takes time to get over the road on your tummy. My mum was very embarrassed.

Most dogs I know like playing with balls, I love sticks, the bigger the better. I steal socks and hide them.

I once stole my grandfather's boxer shorts while he was in the shower, followed by his towel so he was stranded in the bathroom until my grandma went to rescue him with another towel.

I love being a spaniel and I am so lucky to have a mum that loves me as much as I love her

My name is Happy and I live in Brussels, Belgium

I love to steal my mum's socks and underwear!

Name	Happy
Birthdate	01/05/2010
My Mum	Viviane
I live in	Tervuren, near Brussels in Belgium
My favourite toy	my many balls in the garden and in the house
I sleep	with my Mum on her bed
Favourite treat	thinly sliced smoked ham, speciality of local butcher
Other favourite treat	a wine gum - but Mum says it's bad for my teeth so I don't get many
Good habits	I get a dentastick after our long morning walk, it cleans my teeth
Bad habits	I steal my Mum's socks and underwear
Other bad habits	I steal Mum's paper hanky wherever I can find it and love shredding it. I sometimes wake her up a bit too early but I cannot help that I just want to give her cuddles and licks when I'm wide awake!
Favourite walk	Tervuren Park & wood. Here I meet plenty of other dogs and there is loads of sniffing to do!
Favourite activity	riding in the car when the roof is down and the wind blowing around me
My friends	every day I meet Starsky & Hutch, two brothers, border collies who wait for me so we can play with the ball or just generally talk about other dogs. I'm their favourite! My human best friend, after my Mum is Oma (my Mum's mum) where I stay when my Mum has to go away for work. She always has plenty of treats. We cook together and go for long walks. She is slower so I have to be on best behaviour, but I don't mind as she is always introducing me to friends of hers who then admire me

Bonjour!

My name is Happy and I live with my Mum Viviane in Tervuren near Brussels, Belgium. I just love cars. My first memory of cars is actually when my Mum came to collect me to go to my forever home. I was a bit afraid as I did not know her that well. She took me to this big shiny box, stepped in and settled me on her lap. I was more curious than afraid and of course, I got lots of cuddles on that first car experience. I was the cutest puppy! I soon came to think of cars as fun places to be.

I was a bit pig-headed to start with and did not want to sit alone in the back. I definitely did not like the harness my Mum used to strap me in with! So, I managed to gnaw my way through 3 harnesses. She finally got the message and let me sit next to her up front. Mind you, she's clever my Mum, soon I had to admit she was right, when on a couple of occasions I slid off the seat when she had to brake. I soon learned my lesson and now actually enjoy sitting on the back seat with my driver up front!

I have taught my Mum to crack the window open on the passenger side when we are driving slowly, usually on the last stretch home. I stand with my front paws on the armrest and look intently at the button she has to push. She quickly got the message, I've trained her well.

What I like best about being in the car with my mum is when she opens the roof. She's got this dinky sports car and I sit in the back, enjoying the wind through my hair, with my ears flapping away! Oh my, what a great feeling. I get a lot of admiring looks from people in other cars. True, I'm a bit of a diva, but can I help it that people think I'm cute. They come up to me and say "hello" when I'm waiting in the car for my Mum, while she is out shopping for my favourite treats and stuff for her.

I love my Mum, and her mum, Oma (Gran in Flemish) is also a very nice lady who spoils me rotten when I go and stay with her. I think my Mum loves me too, as she is always whispering in my ear when I sit on her lap. She bangs on this weird contraption she calls her computer in her office. Sometimes I'm bored with her working all day and so I climb on her lap for a cuddle or a treat. I do love it when she takes me on appointments with her and I get to meet new people.

My doggie life is a good life, I feel I'm blessed with a nice home, all the food I like, a big garden to play in and loads of toys, treats and cuddles. What more can a dog ask for?

My name is Hudson, I live in Fife, Scotland

My dad says I have cloth ears as I don't listen to him - but I do listen to my mum!!

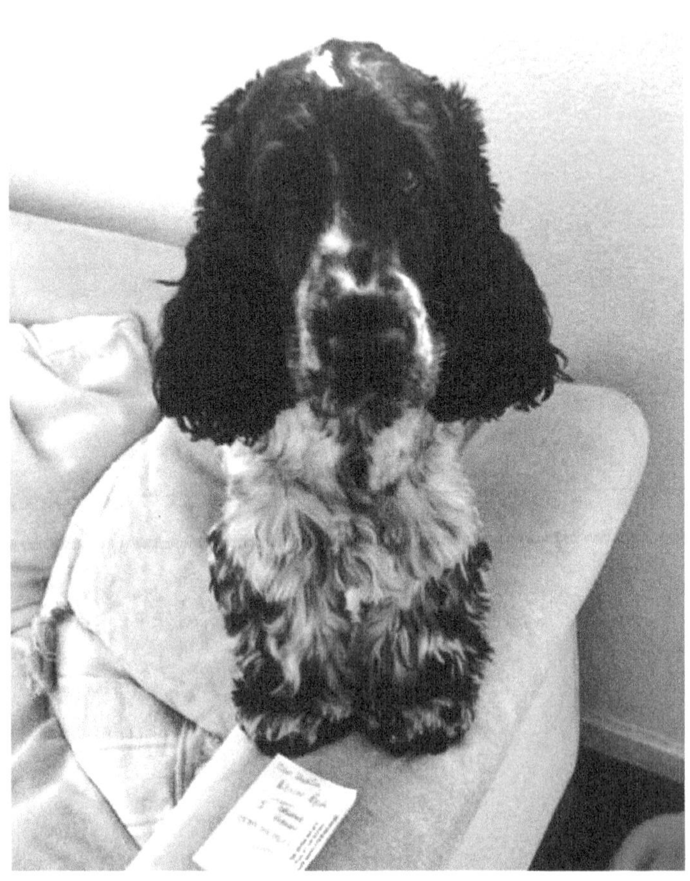

Name	Hudson
Birthdate	02/02/2008
My Mum and Dad	Kylie & Craig
I live in	Fife, Scotland
My favourite toy	I love teddies and soft toys but my brother Bailey kills them all.
I sleep	In my bed next to Mummy's side of the bed. I sometimes sneak up for a snuggle on their bed too.
Favourite treat	I love frozen duck necks to keep my teeth nice and clean and anything Daddy sneaks us out of the fridge.
Other favourite treat	I love raw carrot and the odd sneaky digestive biscuit
Good habits	Mum says my best habit is that I'm a Mummy's boy and love cuddles with anyone who will let me! I'm very quiet and not a hyper cocker. I love to snuggle up on the sofa and have my humans with me.
Bad habits	Dad says I have cloth ears; I don't listen to him when he talks to me but I listen to my mummy!
Other bad habits	When Mum & Dad get our harnesses out to take me for a walk, I get so excited that I can't sit still for them to put it on and I squeal with giddiness
Favourite walk	Bailey and I love Loch Leven and St Andrews beach. I like to do a runner on the beach at St Andrews.
Favourite activity	Cuddles with my humans and playing Toro the Bull with Bailey. I LOVE playing in the snow.
My friends	I suppose I should say Bailey. Sigh, he can be a pest.

I was almost 5 months old when I was taken to my forever home

Mum and Dad brought me home a little bit later than most puppies, I was almost 5 months old when they took me to my forever home and I've been their pride and joy ever since (obviously!!). They think they struck lucky with me because I was never a chewer (well, apart from the time I took offence at the newly laid hallway carpet and helpfully ripped it up, oh, and the time I snuck into Daddy's office as a pup and made confetti out of his papers), I don't

bark a lot (unless it's the posty, or as I call him, 'He who must be barked at'), and I absolutely love, love, love having snuggles with Mum & Dad.

When Mum & Dad brought me home, my breeder told them that I was just finding my bark. Well, it took quite a while for my bark to come, but instead, I found that I was good at singing. I used to sing at every opportunity to my Mummy, especially if she was holding an empty toilet roll, I love those, Daddy used to record me and then they would watch the video and laugh. I don't see why it's funny, I think I should be on Britain's Got Spaniel Talent; I could go all the way you know. But apart from my singing, I didn't really bark very much.

One day my Mummy came home from work and was calling for me and I didn't come running to the door to greet her like I normally do. She hunted all over the house and was shouting and shouting and still I didn't make a sound. By this point, Mummy sounded quite upset and I heard her phone my Daddy and tell him that I must have been stolen as she couldn't find me. Still, I didn't let out a peep. Eventually (stupid Mum), she came back to the bathroom door which she'd previously just poked her head around before closing the door again to double check everywhere and as she opened the door I sprang out!! Surprise!!! I'd snuck in during the day and the door had closed behind me, and because I didn't really do barking back then, I just waited for Mummy to come and find me! She was very upset, but I helped her to cheer up by showing her the toilet rolls I'd made confetti with :)

I have a very happy life with my Mum & Dad, I really love human company and as well as my Mum and Dad, I get to have cuddles with my Grannies too, they are brilliant. When they visit they always bring me a toy and a treat. They know to bring me cuddly toys, they are my favourite. Of course, I know that my Grannies are a bit older, so I don't pester them like I do Mum and Dad.

My favourite thing to do with Mummy is to pinch her socks. As soon as she comes in from work, I sit in front of her and give her the look that says 'give me the sock' and lift a paw. Mummy takes her shoes off and starts to take her socks off and then I pull them the rest of the way and scamper off with my prize. In all of my 6 years I've never put a hole in a sock, that's naughty Bailey's domain. And I've never tried one of my Daddy's socks (clean or dirty), I don't like his!

I love to potter in the garden when it's been snowing, I stick my nose down and force my way through the snow and make a path, and I love to roll about in it. And when I come back inside, Mum and Dad dry me off with a warm towel. I am one pampered pooch.

Last year, Mum and Dad started to feel guilty that I spend a few hours a day on my own at home whilst Mum is out at work. They knew how much I love to play with other doggies in the park. Mum decided that they should get a playmate for me so that I wasn't lonely. They knew that they wanted another cocker, and definitely a blue roan like me. Last November, they brought home Bailey Weed (they nicknamed him weed because he grew like one; I won't mention some of his other nicknames!). I was NOT happy with this - he was noisy, had sharp teeth, pinched my toys and took lots of Mum and Dad's attention for a wee while. Plus, he used to make Mummy get up in the night to let him out for wee-wees and that disrupted my beauty sleep, which is frankly not on. Bailey tried to play with me when he was a baby by nipping my legs with his cockerdile teeth and hanging off my ears, but when I used to nip him back, Mum and Dad got upset. It took us a few months to get used to each other but now, a year on, we are the best of buddies. We cuddle up together for naps and Bailey cleans me (that's a bit annoying but I let him do it because he's my brother and I love him).

Mum and Dad have found out this week that Bailey and I have a new game - they are calling me Toro the Bull but I don't know why. Bailey and I circle each other and I swipe my paws across the floor and then we start rolling around on the floor with each other.

We love playing, Mum says it's great because it tuckers
Bailey out and he settles down for a power nap!!

My name is Bailey; I live in Fife, Scotland

I chew EVERYTHING and pinch ANYTHING!

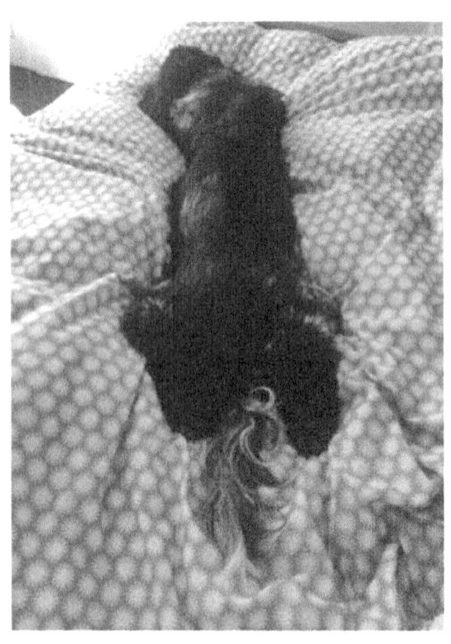

Name	Bailey
Birthdate	13/09/2013
My Mum and Dad	Kylie & Craig
I live in	Fife, Scotland
My favourite toy	Anything I can chew - normally my dumbbell.
I sleep	On Mum & Dad's bed. I force my way between them and spread out like a starfish. They tell me they enjoy hanging off the edge of the bed (I don't understand sarcasm so it must be true!!)
Favourite treat	I love Scruffy Bites and our Daddy sneaks us little bits of cocktail sausages and pretends Mummy doesn't know.
Other favourite treat	Mum gives me raw carrot. I love to chomp them and they keep our teeth sparkly
Good habits	I love to fetch and I sit and lie down and give paws.
Bad habits	Too many to name!! I like to sing and sing whenever my Daddy leaves the room until he comes back. Mummy is not as good as Daddy so I make sure I don't shut up even when Mummy tickles my tummy.
Other bad habits	I chew EVERYTHING and pinch ANYTHING I can get my gnashers on. I am particularly fond of bras and pants; socks have no chance when I am around!
Favourite walk	Mum and Dad take me to Loch Leven a lot, to the nature reserve. My brother Hudson sniffs everywhere and I follow him. He looks after me when we are out.
Favourite activity	Err, eating and chewing of course!!
My friends	My brother Hudson is my best friend. I love him loads. I also really like the hoover

My Mum and Dad brought me home to live with them in November 2013. They had been to see me a few times with my breeder and my cocker Mummy and they were so excited because I'm really cute. They told me all about my big brother Hudson who lived with them, and on the way home from collecting me, we stopped off at my Granny's to say 'hello' as it was a long journey for a little pup. My Granny was really confused, she didn't know that I was coming

to live with them and at first she thought I was Hudson! To let her know I wasn't Hudson, I peed on her carpet and then curled up for a sleep.

Once we got to my forever home, Mum and Dad introduced me to Hudson. I loved him at first sight, I knew my big brother would always look after me (and he has, he is a great big brother) and so I decided to show my love and affection for him by nibbling on his ears and cheekily nipping his legs. I don't think he liked that very much as he kept yelping. Mum and Dad had gotten me a puppy pen to sleep in and have little time outs, so that Hudson could have quiet time with them but once I got used to my new surroundings I decided I didn't like the pen and would whimper and jump up and down to make them let me out. When I was out of my pen, I especially liked to CHEW!! I chewed carpet, walls, Mum's dining table and two of her chairs, I shredded Hudson's soft teddies and I also chewed my puppy food bowl.

After my inoculations, Mum and Dad took me out for my first walk in the outside world. Man, that was SCARY! Everything was so big and colourful. I wasn't sure about the collar and lead and kept yapping at them, and once we got to the park at the end of our street, I kept sitting down and refusing to move. But, lovely Hudson gave me a little nudge and kept looking out to make sure I was nearby and I slowly settled into being out and about. Now, I'm as giddy as Hudson to go out.

In contrast to Hudson, I am 100% a Daddy's boy. My Daddy is the best. Mum is ok as she feeds us and cleans up after us, and so I let her have cuddles with me, but we all really know that Dad is my favourite. If Dad goes to the bathroom, or out of the room, I will lie on my back and have a paddy, I howl and howl until he comes back and then I pretend nothing has happened, and give him a big waggy cocker cuddle. I've also quickly worked out that if I pinch stuff (tea towels, pants, and stones from the garden), under the dining table is a great place to hide my stash, as the humans can't get under there very easily. It also means that Daddy goes to the kitchen and gets me a treat to make me hand over my treasure. It's a win-win situation. I've become particularly adept at pinching Mum's bras and pants from the wash basket. One day, Dad didn't realise that I'd gotten into the wash basket and had snaffled one of Mummy's (new) bras and had shot off into the garden with it. He peered out of one of the upstairs windows to see me tearing round the garden with the bra straps round my neck, dragging it through mud and rolling about, chewing away at it. Mummy wasn't very happy but I just gave her my little cocker wiggle and all was forgiven. I've since done the same with pants and don't get me started on socks!! They are just meant for me to chew. Sometimes, Hudson plays with me and grabs the other end of a sock and we stretch and stretch and stretch them so that they are stretched beyond recognition. I'm very clever that way.

Mum and Dad have recently got new duck feather pillows for their bed. Duck feathers mean DUCKS, and I love ducks. I'm plotting destruction of said pillows.

My name is Bracken, I live in Wiltshire, UK

I like to eat and swallow stones

Name	Bracken (KC name Philelm Robbie)
Birthdate	01/06/2010
My Mum	Kirsa
I live in	Calne, Wiltshire
My favourite toy	a tiny red rubber squeaky ball and a soft pheasant, my mum keeps taking it off me because I keep chewing him up
I sleep	I have two different beds in the kitchen which I alternate between and sometimes I sleep in my bed in front of the log burner in the lounge
Favourite treat	cheese. I also like to drink the tea dregs out of my mum's cup of tea after breakfast
Other favourite treat	doggie chocolate drops every night before bedtime and when my family have to go out and leave me. I jump in my bed, expectantly waiting for them
Good habits	I always sit and wait nicely for my food and don't eat until I'm told. I'm very good at waiting and always stay close to my mum on walks. I am very friendly to everyone and other dogs, even when they are not friendly to me
Bad habits	I have been known to eat stones, which nearly killed me. I also like to steal socks from the washing and tea towels off the side. My family don't have one teacloth without a chewed corner.
Other bad habits	I really like to roll in anything poo related. Badger, fox, bird, I'm not bothered which. I also like to roll in slugs resulting in a very messy jelly coat.
Favourite walk	Wiltshire Downs and along the ridgeway. Savernake forest, Bowood estate, Lulworth cove. The beaches of Polzeath, Perranporth and Hayle
Favourite activity	Chasing bubbles in the garden. Getting wet and muddy, chasing pheasants. Lots of cuddles with mum
My friends	Jenson a Rottweiler, Oakley and Libby the labs. Poppy a Jack Russell and Daisy a Westie. My mum is my best friend. I love my dad Simon and sister Harriet. I am friends with Yoda the hamster. I love to stay at grandma and grampy's house when my family have to go away.

Hello, my name is Bracken and I live with my mum Kirsa, my dad Simon and sister Harriet in Calne, Wiltshire. I was born in Warminster, Wiltshire where I lived with my working cocker family until my human family bought me from a reputable breeder and bought me home 8 weeks later.

I was a really good puppy and my mum thought it would be a good idea to crate me from the start as their other dog (Oliver the chocolate Labrador who had sadly passed away) had destroyed their kitchen with chewing. I didn't mind, I loved my crate and found it very secure. However on the first night I was separated from my cocker family I was a bit sad and cried. My new mum knew that she shouldn't give in to my cries and ignored me all night until about 5am when she couldn't stand it anymore and came down to see me. However she was horrified when she'd discovered the reason I'd been crying so much was because I'd tipped my water bowl all over me and I was soaking wet. She did feel guilty! Never mind, she soon learned that lesson and the water didn't appear in my crate again. I now have two really comfy beds to choose from in the kitchen and no longer have a crate as I'm such a good boy, but I do have a travel crate for the car which I love going in.

My mum and dad always take me away on holiday with them when they can. I had my first holiday when I was only 12 weeks old. However, it cost them a fortune in parking fees as they always needed an hour longer, as it would take them twice as long to get around anywhere. Everyone kept stopping to make a fuss of me as I was so cute! We have enjoyed holidays in Hampshire, Dorset, Northumbria and the Scottish highlands. My favourite place of all is in Cornwall, where we go regularly, as my Grandma and Grampy have a holiday home there. I just absolutely love running on the beaches and frolicking in the sea.

I'm a bit of an accident prone cocker I'm afraid!

I seem to find life far too interesting and seem to end up in several scrapes. My first little accident was when my dad took me for a rare walk with my sister Harriet. I say rare, only because it's normally mum's job to walk me. Mum had to go out, it was the Sunday before Christmas and she needed to buy some stocking fillers for us. We got home and mum had literally walked through the door to be met with shouts of "ring the vets"! Turns out I'd cut my tummy open on some barbed wired even though I hadn't noticed. It was a Sunday and we had to drive over to the big hospital in the next town where they'd decided the cut was too deep and I needed to be put out while I was stitched back up again. It actually worked out in my favour as unbeknown to me, mum had booked me in to have a little operation to remove something called "bits", I didn't like the sound of this but my escapade with the barbed wire meant this was postponed. Sadly though, I found out I was to have this operation rebooked for my 1st birthday! I have forgiven mum as she gave me lots and lots of cuddles.

One winter we were out walking near our home in some fields and I disappeared. I don't normally go very far from mum, but I'd gone into a wooded area and although I wasn't far, mum couldn't find me. She called and called and I could tell she was panicking but I couldn't get back to her. You see, what mum didn't know, is that I'd wandered onto a deep pond that was covered in this funny hard white stuff. I must have thought it was fun at first, but then I got to the middle and fell through. I tried and tried to climb out but it was just too slippery for me to get a grip and I kept sliding back underneath. Just then my mum spotted me and I could tell she looked really scared. She stepped onto this white stuff (which I later found out was something called ice) and straight away she too fell through and got wet. My mum was really scared now, as she knew she shouldn't have done that and she's not a very good swimmer but I knew she was desperate to save me. I was getting so tired and I didn't have much strength left to keep holding myself up. Mum called for help but no one came. She called again and some school children came on their bikes and they were brilliant. Between them they found a really big stick and slid it onto the ice and I managed to hook my paws onto it while they pulled me out. Mum was so relieved she cried but when she got home and told dad what happened, he was very cross, but I think that was because he was worried as both me and mum were cold and wet.

When I was younger I also had a bad habit of eating things I shouldn't, everything from different types of poo, to dead animals or live ones for that matter! I have swallowed dead mice and birds which have made me very sick. I have, on more than one occasion, been very proud of myself when I've found dead rabbits. I presented them to my mum but I couldn't understand why mum wasn't very pleased. I later heard her telling dad that the rabbits were rancid, black and crawling with maggots! I have also killed two other rabbits by chasing and catching them. Although I'm a working cocker, I'm not trained as a worker

and didn't know what to do, but mum understood this was my instinct. I also once found a very interesting slimy creature which hopped about on our patio, I thought it was dinner so swallowed it whole! It was a bit wriggly as I tried to swallow it but it was a treat. I didn't understand why Mum was so worried, she told dad that frogs or toads were poisonous to dogs and she sat up all night with me in case I was poorly, but luckily I was fine.

My biggest concern to my family is that I like to eat and swallow stones. I have done this a lot, but have passed them out of my system. On four occasions it has resulted in a trip to the vets. Each time this was on a Sunday or bank holiday and on one occasion right in the middle of the royal wedding, I wasn't fussy when I did it! But the last time it happened mum just knew something was seriously wrong. I was not myself at all. Even though mum didn't know I'd eaten anything bad, she just knew something was wrong and insisted I went to the vets. Mum and dad took me and the vet looked really worried. She first thought it was pancreatitis, but after an x-ray discovered, I'd swallowed a really big stone that had become stuck. She told mum and dad they needed to operate straight away or I could die; she also said I may not even make it through the operation. I was only four and didn't want to die. My mum was heartbroken, she had to quickly say goodbye to me and was crying. Later that night, the vet rang them and told them I'd made it through the operation, but that it was still touch and go, that my stomach juices may leak and this could still kill me. They told her it was a 50/50 chance and that I'd probably need to be in hospital for about 7 days. Mum didn't sleep a wink all night and she just kept praying hard for me. The next evening the vet phoned home and asked my family if they could come and pick me up as I was more alert and awake than I should be! I was very sore but the relief when I saw my family was immense. My mum hugged me and cried again when she saw me! I have to be really, really careful now, as I was told if it happens again my chances are even slimmer.

I am a very lucky boy as I'm blessed with a family that love me and do fun things with me. I have lots of nice doggy friends and human friends too! I am very affectionate and always happy and my tail is always wagging; my family say if they could harness the energy in my tail they'd have free power!

My name is Darcy, I live in Scarborough, UK

My mum and I were once airlifted off a cliff by our local Coastguards. It was shown on the TV that evening!

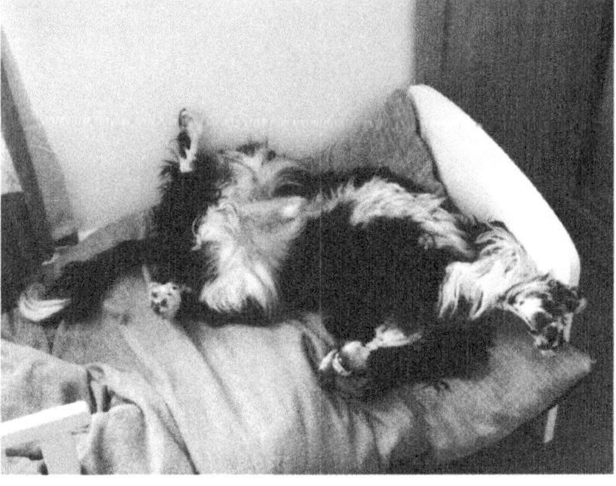

Name	Darcy
Birthdate	29/04/2008
My Mum	Tracy
I live in	Scarborough
My favourite toy	anything soft
I sleep	in mum's bedroom; I have my own human bed in there
Favourite treat	cheese
Other favourite treat	sausages
Good habits	I can be left alone in the house without doing anything naughty to it. I can also be let off my lead around people and dogs now. I used to run off and jump on them. Now I just run off, say hello and come back.
Bad habits	I bark in the car all the way to where I'm going. I also bark at other dogs when I'm on the lead. (I only want to play)
Favourite walk	in the woods and the beach
Favourite activity	bringing shoes to people when they come to my house.
My friends	I have lots of friends. I have a little sister called Dotty. I have a girlfriend called Sadie who I see about twice a week. Charlie who lives with my Nan.
My human friends	I have my mum whom I love lots. My dad and two big sisters who adore me and I adore them in turn. When they have to go to their mum's house, I don't see them for three days. They always come back and make a big fuss of me.

Hi, my name is Darcy and I am a 6 and a half year old sprocker spaniel. My mum was looking for a dog when she came across an advert from a lady that couldn't cope with me. My mum and Nan came to meet me and I think my mum would call our first meeting 'A little chaotic'! I couldn't contain myself with excitement when they came into the room to meet me. I wanted to give them a big welcome and jumped onto them both. Unfortunately my Nan went flying off the chair when I jumped onto her! I decided I had better be good for a minute, so I lay down on the floor for a short while and then jumped onto my Nan again whereby she went flying off the chair again. You would have thought she would have tried harder to stay on the chair a second time... My mum thought I was crazy and fell in love with me, the feeling was mutual and she took me home with her to live near the beach in Scarborough.

One of my finest moments was when I was on television wagging my tail while my mum was being airlifted off the cliff in the background by our local coastguards. I don't think my mum sees this as her finest moment!

It all happened so quickly, I was running around minding my own business, sniffing out scents as a sprocker does. Next minute I seemed to be halfway up the cliff and couldn't get down. I was stuck. My mum seemed to be panicking a lot and shouting at me, but however much she shouted, it didn't change the fact that I was stuck. My mum wanted me to come back down the way I had gone up, but that was a lot easier said than done. The best part of the game was when my mum climbed up the cliff to join me. But rather than join me, she went a different route to the top and then started shouting at me again to come to her. (Another one of her bright ideas!) I was still stuck so decided to stay where I was. My mum then decided finally to come and join me on my ledge, which was great, but then we were both stuck. She then slid about 4 feet down the cliff. I wished she would make up her mind; she was either up the top or sliding down past me! Someone heard my mum scream and shouted at her that the coastguard had been rung. When they arrived, they were very kind enough to air lift me and my mum to the top of the cliff. Hence my mum watching us on the TV that night!

One night my mum was having a bath and went under the water and shut her eyes. I choose this moment to jump on her and give her some kisses. She started making a right noise, screaming and spluttering. I think she got some water in her mouth when she screamed. Silly mummy! When she came up out of the water she was choking away, she looked shocked and surprised to see me sat in the other end of the bath wagging my tail.

My name is Molly, I live in Newcastle, UK

My motto is 'Never bet on a spaniel, they will win every time'

Name	Molly
Birthdate	18/11/2009
My Mum and Dad	Ami & Andy
I live in	Newcastle, United Kingdom
My favourite toy	Tennis Ball and my ball launcher
I sleep	with my mum and dad. I sleep all afternoon after my walks with my dog walker Sarah. I like to sleep with my Aunty Kate when she sleeps over, but I have to wait until she is asleep before sneaking into the bed.
Favourite treat	Chicken and gravy dinner when I visit my nana on Sunday.
Other favourite treat	anything available when I put on my puppy dog eyes, works every time.
Good habits	I am a springer spaniel - do we have any?! My mum and dad say I'm a princess and I am always good for them but other people think I'm mad as a hatter
Bad habits	I sometimes get mud or sand on the bed after my walks. My mum keeps saying things like "I am fed up with changing this bed." She sometimes closes the door but I am such a clever girl I can open it now!
Other bad habits	I love water and mud. My granddad once said to my nana, "I bet she will not get too wet in that puddle, it's not deep enough". I proved him wrong because I lay down and rolled in it. My motto is never bet on a spaniel, they will win every time.
Favourite walk	Rising Sun Country Park or any beach. I also love my walks with all my doggy friends who come on walks with me and my dog walker, Sarah.
Favourite activity	watching for those four legged, furry things. I think they are called cats. My nana calls me meerkat Molly as I am always looking out of the windows for pesky cats. My nana has a cat friend called Mouse; he is the neighbour's cat. I am not happy about this and will catch him one day but he is too fast for me at the moment. My nana warns him when I'm coming which is really mean.

My friends	I have lots of friends. Ruby, Alfie, Milly, Daisy, Dani, Snoopy, Jack, Pepper and Sam, who like to join me and my dog walker Sarah on our daily walks. We all like to play chase together which means I get a lot of exercise which is great for me. I am the only springer Spaniel and I am faster than all my friends, so I always get the ball first. I sometimes get to ride in the van's passenger seat next to Sarah. I love this, as I get extra treats, but we all have to take it in turns, so I sometimes have to go in a cage at the back. We all get on really well.

Let me introduce myself - my name is Molly!

My name WAS Marley, but when I was 5 months old my owners realised that with 2 small children, I was probably not the best breed of dog to have. I was very nervous because there was a lot of shouting and noise in the house.

One day my now Nana Lynda came and fell in love with me, well who wouldn't, she let me out of my bed and stroked me and said I was so cute. I liked her a lot cos she was the kindest person I had met even though I was a bit nervous and weed on her shoe… oops! Well, it turned out nana Lynda's daughter Ami and her boyfriend Andy were looking for a dog and my nana persuaded them to have me, I think I hit the jackpot that day.

Nana Lynda came back for me and put me in her car, I was so excited to get out of the house I weed all over the car! She did not shout at me, which was a bit strange cos everyone else did. I met Ami and Andy and they loved me too, I was on a roll with my cuteness, but still weeing everywhere!.

I gave them a few sad puppy eye looks and that was it, I was going to be their new dog. I was very nervous and when they got me home, I weed all over, I was just so excited cos they kept stroking me and cuddling me. They put me in a cage on my first night, saying no dogs in the bed. Well, I put paid to that: I cried all night, it worked cos they felt sorry for me, let me in the bed and yes you have guessed it, after 5 years, I am the queen of the bed and let them in, they take up a lot of space but I love them, so its fine.

Well that's how I ended up being nana Lynda's grandog; she loves and spoils me a lot, I love going for Sunday dinner, she makes the best dinners full of veg, meat and yummy gravy. I remember the first time I went, I did not know the joint of lamb was for everyone, so I jumped up on the table thingy and ate it all when they were busy talking, they all just laughed at me… uhmmm … humans can be strange creatures.

When I go to my nanas there are a lot of cats around outside, but I keep watch out the window; they laugh and call me Meerkat Molly, they are a strange bunch. I get lots of attention, but just lately I have heard my nana talking about Mouse who comes to see her, he is the neighbour's cat and he is very old. I think nana likes him a lot cos there are cat treats and new food bowls next to mine, I do not like sharing my nana, so I am now on a mission to scare him away but even though he is old he can run faster than me and I am a springer. He always gets away, the little blighter, sometimes nana tells him I am coming and sends him home before I get there; she is a spoil sport.

One day Mousy boy, one day!

I love my walks and I live next to a country park, so it's open the door and off I go, no leader, no cars, just me, mam, dad and the great outdoors, we have great fun and walk for miles, well they walk, I run cos I am the fastest dog in town.

I often smell some funny things, I think the humans call them foxes, they leave funny brown things on the grass and I love to roll in them, my dad does not like it and tells me off, but then gives me nice bath and I smell really nice, there is method to my madness you know, it works every time. I love my bath time, but dad just thinks I am a naughty girl!

I have a ball and it's all mine and I am very touchy about other dogs and sometime I snap a bit, well why should I share, it's all mine. One day my mam had one of her very bad ideas and thought it would be good to have a dog walker to help me be more social with other dogs.

Sarah came for a visit and she was so nice so I thought, ok I like the sound of this. Well I found out the truth when she came back, I was jumping all over with excitement, but when we got outside she put me in a van thingy and I could see other dogs, well this was new and I was not sure I liked it.

We all got out and ran around for hours, it was great fun, but I had a few moments when the other dogs were being naughty, so I put them in their place. After all this was my dog walker and remember, I do not share. Over the next few weeks and with Sarah's patience, love and guidance, I am slowly learning to share and now love all my fur friends. I even have a special friend Snoopy, I share a cage with him, he is so cute!

Well that's some of my story; I have lots of tales to tell, but wanted you all to know that I am the happiest springer in the world with my forever family. If I was human, it would feel like I had won that lottery thing humans always wish they could win.

I hope you enjoy all our stories and anyone reading this book, anyone who does not have a springer spaniel: we are simply the best dogs in the whole world! We are funny, adorable, naughty and very mucky, but have lots of love to give and just want to be loved in return.

I have the best family who love me and call me Princess Molly cos I have to be the centre of attention, but that's what springers are all about.

Woof for now! Love, Princess Molly

My name is Kes, I live in Brighton, West Sussex, UK

My favourite thing in the whole wide world is my tennis ball

Name	Kes
Birthdate	16/08/2010
My Mum	Laura
I live in	Brighton, West Sussex UK
My favourite toy	Always a tennis ball
I sleep	with my little sister Kao in our own doggy room
Favourite treat	Chicken and tuna
Other favourite treat	anything that mum and dad are eating!
Good habits	I get a dental stick every day when my mum and dad have their dinner. If my little sister Kao gets lost on a walk, I go and find her and bring her back to daddy.
Bad habits	I always tease my little sister Kao with a toy and then we both get into trouble when we fight over it. I also sit on human people's feet so that they have to pay attention to me and stroke me.
Other bad habits	when I don't want to do anything I roll over on my back and flash my tummy. Sometimes when daddy is on the sofa, I will paw his arm constantly as he is paying too much attention to the television and not enough attention to me.
Favourite walk	South Downs
Favourite activity	Going to agility training and entering competitions with my dad. I love chasing tennis balls. Daddy will hide a tennis ball and send me off to find it. Silly daddy for losing the ball.
My friends	My mate Kye and my little sister Kao. I love everyone I see and meet wherever I go. I really love my human friend David, Mummy and Daddy's son. Every time I see him I pee myself with excitement.

My name is Kes and I live with my mommy and daddy in a small village in West Sussex, England.

My favourite thing in the whole wide world is my tennis ball. One day when we were out in the woods daddy went off and left me by the side of the field just outside of the trees. I was not very happy because daddy told me to stay where I was and not to move while he went off with my tennis ball and played with it all on his own. I wanted to go running after him as it was my ball, not his!!

I did as I was told and stayed where I was, as I wanted to be good for daddy. Daddy came back to me a minute later, although it felt like it was taking him forever to return. When he did come back to me he had lost my ball. Silly daddy! My ball! MY BALL!! Not daddy's ball.

I was so upset and worried, I started to panic. This was my favourite tennis ball, even though I have hundreds of balls at home; this one was truly my favourite. I did not know that daddy had been playing a new game with me. This new game was called "go find". I think the idea was for me to go find the tennis ball. Daddy did try to help me a little bit to find it, but in the end daddy was just too slow. I went running off into the woods and after a little bit of sniffing here and a little bit there I found it. YIPEE!! I found my ball. Silly daddy, you are not getting my ball back ever again.

Daddy and I play this "go find" game all the time now. I love this game. I am so good at it now, that if anyone else is silly enough to lose their ball, daddy will tell me to go find theirs too and I find it. I can even find it the day after daddy has lost it the day before.

This is proving to be a very good game, as I find so many lost balls. Mommy and daddy collect them all together and in June mommy will wash them all in the big scary washing machine and then dry them in the even bigger scarier drying machine, to get them all nice and smelly clean. We then meet up with my puppies every year and take all the nice clean balls with us on our annual puppy walk and give all the previously found tennis balls to everyone we meet on our walk.

Now there are no lost balls and on that one day in June everyone is playing the "go find" game.

Another game I play with daddy is "agility". Daddy and I have had to train very hard to play this game and I truly love it. We go to special places called "shows" and we get to play this game alongside lots of other doggies, who are all shapes and sizes. I must be getting quite good at this game as daddy has been given lots of trophies and rosettes and prizes when we play. Daddy gives me lots of hugs and kisses when I play this game properly.

Sometimes I don't want to play, so when I don't feel like playing I will just go and lie down, roll over and flash my tummy to everyone. This makes everyone laugh and chuckle although sometimes not daddy. The people who make sure that I play this game perfectly, called the "judges", will laugh at me too.

I like to make people laugh and it's good for me too, because when everyone laughs, I also get a tummy tickle and daddy gives the best tummy tickles ever.

From walkies each day and agility at the weekends, every day is a mini adventure.

My name is Kao, I live in Brighton, West Sussex, UK

I love to swim with Mummy and Daddy in their Jacuzzi

Name	Kao
Birthdate	14/09/13
My Mum	Laura
I live in	Brighton, West Sussex UK
My favourite toy	anything I can get my teeth on, I really love tennis balls
I sleep	with my big sister Kes in our own doggy room
Favourite treat	Cooked chicken and doggy sausages
Other favourite treat	anything that mum and dad are eating!
Good habits	I get a dental stick every day when my mum and dad have their dinner. I give great hugs and kisses
Bad habits	I always take my mum's shoes before she can put them on to go to work. I am also rather partial to socks. When I am out on walks I love to roll in fox poo. When I am in the garden, I like to bring my mum in a nice shiny stone.
Other bad habits	chewing everything! The skirting boards and hall rug are my favourite at the moment.
Favourite walk	South Downs
Favourite activity	going for long walks and chasing tennis balls or rabbits. I also love my agility training.
My friends	My big sister Kes and big brother Kye. My best friend ever is Morphy the pussy cat.

I love to run. I love to play catch. I love to go walkies. I love to play in the garden. I love water. I really love water!!

Mommy says I am not allowed in the bathroom when she has the water in the big shiny white thing with all the bubbles in it. I have been in there with the bubbles, when mommy didn't see me. It was fun to eat the bubbles and play in there, but mommy was not very happy when I did this, so that place is out of bounds now!

I have now found another place where I can go. Mommy and daddy have a big container of water outside in the garden, called a "Jacuzzi". I like the Jacuzzi. It's lovely and warm and I can go swimming in there. I try to go swimming even when mommy and daddy are in there. It's fun and it's so funny when mommy and daddy tell me to stop swimming or when we play a game where I try to jump in to swim and mommy has to catch me before I do. Silly mommy, I'm too quick, she can't catch me, nah nah! Now mommy and daddy tell me to wait in the house when they want to go swimming. That's OK because I can play with my best friend Morphy.

Morphy is a little bit smaller than me but he is really fast. We like to play chase. Sometimes I chase Morphy and sometimes Morphy will chase me. This is a game we play a lot. Sometimes mommy or daddy will tell us to stop playing, as we are both getting too tired. Sometimes when I catch Morphy he makes a funny sound. It's not like the sound I make when Morphy catches me, my sound is "woof woof", Morphy's sound is "hiss hiss" or "meow meow" (you've guessed it, he's my cat brother!).

When we don't play chase, we snuggle up together on the sofa or on the floor. It's nice to snuggle with Morphy as he is nice and warm and really soft. When we snuggle, Morphy will hold onto my paw and this makes me feel nice and safe. Sometimes, when I wake up, Morphy will wash my face with his funny sticky tongue and he won't let me go away until he has finished. It feels really funny when he does this, but I don't mind. I share my dinner with him too and if he's not hungry, I get to eat his dinner, but I have to get in there quick before my big sister Kes or my big brother Kye eats it.

I love my brother and sister. We play all the time. It's fun to get all the toys out of the toy box and play tug and chase. We have lots of toys to play with, but when my brother or my sister has a toy, why is it always the toy that I wanted to play with. That's OK, because if I'm quick and sneaky, I can usually get the toy back.

Mommy says I have to learn to share, and to slow down and to play nicely but there's just too much to fit into one day. One thing that I know I can do is give the best ever hugs and kisses in the whole wide world. Mommy also gives me lots of hugs and kisses especially when we are out "training".

I am learning just like my big sister Kes to do "agility training".

Even though my mommy says I am a handful she also says, that she has never, ever laughed so much with a puppy, than how she does with me!

YIPEE!! I make my mommy smile and laugh.

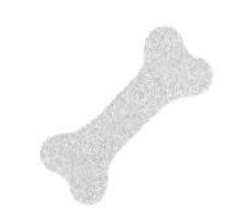

My Name is Kye, I live in Brighton, West Sussex, UK

I love to steal the cat's dinner or anyone else's I can get my spaniel chops on!

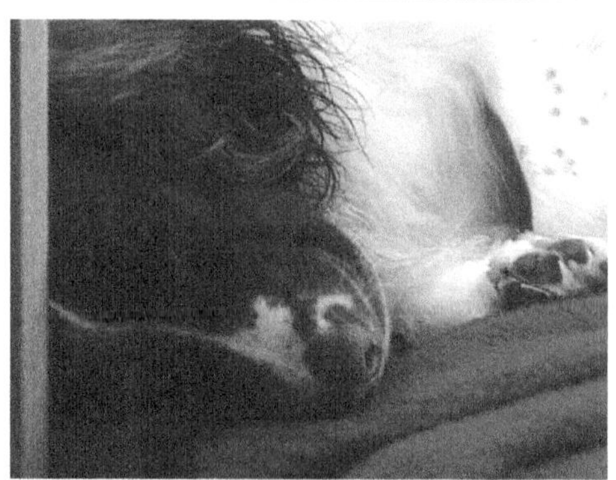

Name	Kye
Birthdate	10/06/11
My Mum	Laura
I live in	Brighton, West Sussex UK
My favourite toy	I don't play with toys often as I am always tired. When I do I will share a toy bone with my little sister Kao. We like to play fight over it for a while.
I sleep	upstairs with my mum and dad. I have seizures and they need to be near me when I have one.
Favourite treat	Cheese spread, chicken and ham.
Other favourite treat	Peanut butter and apples. My mum gives me this special treat before I go to bed to keep my sugar levels up throughout the night.
Good habits	I get a dental stick every day when my mum and dad have their dinner. I give amazing hugs.
Bad habits	I always pull on the lead when I'm out with my dad
Other bad habits	I always try and steal the cat's dinner or anyone else's dinner. The medicine I am on makes me feel hungry all the time
Favourite walk	South Downs and the beach
Favourite activity	running in the fields chasing the birds and rabbits
My friends	my mate Kes and little sister Kao.

My mommy and daddy say I am not like other doggies they know, who are the same breed as me

I am an English springer spaniel and mommy says I am a very "special" boy.

I am quiet and calm and very obedient, which everyone says is not like many others of my breed.

Some days it's hard for me to get up in the mornings as I don't always feel too good. I try and feel well all the time as I know this makes my mommy very happy, but when I feel bad, it makes mommy very sad and she worries about me.

Every day I have to take lots of medicine to try and make me feel better. I have to be very careful with what foods I eat and I also have to eat lots of vegetables. I like most vegetables, but mommy keeps giving me these things called "carrots" in my breakfast and dinner. I don't like "carrots" but mommy will insist on putting them in my dish. I am so smart; I can eat everything up and leave the horrible "carrots" all alone in the dish for my sister Kao to eat. No matter how hard mommy tries to hide them, I can still find them, no matter how well hidden, or how small mommy makes them! Silly mommy!!

I think mommy thinks that, if I eat my "carrots", it will make me feel better and I will not have these horrible things, called "seizures". I don't like these "seizures", they are nasty and make me feel so bad. One time I had to go to a special hospital, to see if they could make them go away. I missed mommy and daddy, as I was there a long time and I was so ill. I had to fight and fight to get better again, because I was not ready to go to Rainbow Bridge and leave mommy and daddy alone. This is why mommy says I am her "special" boy. When I came out of hospital, I could not walk, eat or play. It took a long time to feel a little bit better again, now most days I feel good. I am still very wobbly and I shake and have funny little body tremors. I always bump into things, as my spatial awareness has been compromised. Mommy and daddy say they can't wrap me up in cotton wool and I have to be allowed to still be a dog! When I go running in the fields and the woods, you would not know that I am ill, except when I fall over or bump into a silly tree that got in the way.

Every morning mommy will take me with her to feed the fishes. This is a special treat for me because when I go to see the fishes, it is when I know I will have a good day and mommy will smile and be happy, because somehow she knows that too.

My name is Daisy, I live in Warrington, UK

I like to jump on your knee and wrap my paws round your neck for a hug!

Name	Daisy
Birthdate	14/02/2008
My Mum and Dad	Carol and Phil
I live	Lowton near Warrington
My favourite toy	I don't play with toys, but I love my Kong stuffed with banana
I sleep with	my Mum and dad on their bed, with my sister Miffy
Favourite treat	a juicy bone
Other favourite treat	chicken wing or a sneaky piece of cheese
Good habits	I have a raw diet and eat better than my mum and dad
Bad habits	Sitting outside in the rain, just to get wet and make the floors all wet
Other bad habits	Standing under the bush in the garden when it's raining, tickling my back and getting wet
Favourite walk	The beach is my favourite walk, I run around with Miffy barking for no reasons and to let people know it's our beach!
Favourite activity	My favourite activity is to watch Miffy doing all the work to get the treats out of the activity game and I pinch all the treats before Miffy gets to them!
My friends	I'm a bit choosy about the dogs I talk with when I'm out on my walks with my dad, I like to bark at big dogs especially, when I have my pink coat on and show up my dad! I suffer with little dog syndrome! I love all the dogs once I'm off my lead on the field. When dogs come to stay, I'm often grumpy on the first day, I just like to let them know it's my house, but then I'm their best friend by the time they go home. My Human best friend is my daddy's girl and Miffy is mummy's girl. I too love granny, she calls me her grandog as well. I also love the meat man (my mum's dad), he's a butcher and brings us fresh bones. We stay at Mum's friends at Galliano's house, when mummy and daddy are away, they love us there. I'm very quiet compared to mad Miffy and quite like my own company and sleeping on the bed. I love all humans, especially having cuddles, I like to jump on your knee and wrap my paws round your neck for a hug!

My name is Daisy, I am a jet black cocker spaniel and I live in Lowton with my mummy, daddy and my sister Miffy.

I came to live with my new family three years ago when I was 4. When they came to get me, they took me for a walk in the park, well they tried to, I kept sitting down and refusing to move. I think they were worried that I would be scared about leaving with them, but I really liked sitting on my new mummy's lap in the front of the car and looking out of the window. I like lots of hugs and I like giving kisses. I love going for walkies and I get really excited if anyone says the "W" word or if I see someone picking up my lead. I settled in really quickly at my new home with my new sister Miffy. I try to help her stay out of trouble, but she just can't help herself!

My favourite things are singing along to video clips of wolves howling on YouTube, going for long walks and chasing birds. In summer I like chasing the swifts around the local field. They zip around about a foot above the grass and I love chasing them around and around. Sometimes I get so distracted I can't hear my Daddy calling me back and he has to come and get me!

I love going to the beach, I get so excited, I bark at everything and I run into the water and paddle in the waves. One time on the beach, I was chasing seagulls and I found a seagull sat on the sand and it didn't fly away. I stood and looked at it but it didn't look very well, so I gave it a kiss, then I chased after Miffy. I can be grumpy and I don't like change at first, until I have had time to get used to it. I like to bark and growl at anyone who comes to the door. I am always the first to the door to greet mummy and daddy when they get home. One time I was in the garden with daddy, when the next door neighbour was on his conservatory roof fixing his guttering. I thought he was too close to my mummy and daddy's garden so I growled at him to let him know I was keeping my eye on him. But he seemed to think this was funny, because my growl went up and down like a ghost wail! Charming!

My name is Miffy, I live in Warrington, UK

Name	Miffy
Birthdate	13/05/2008
My Mum and Dad	Carol and Phil
I live in	Lowton near Warrington
My favourite toy	My ropey and teddy, also anything that has stuffing in it!
I sleep	With my mum and dad on their bed with my sister Daisy
Favourite treat	a juicy bone or crunchy carrot
Other favourite treat	anything edible I can get my paws on
Good habits	I have a raw diet and eat better than my mum and dad
Bad habits	I steal anything at my height.
Other bad habits	I love to rip up tissues and I'll find tissues where you never knew you had tissues.
Favourite walk	The beach is my favourite walk, I run around with Daisy barking for no reason and to let the other people know it is our beach
Favourite activity	My activity toy which my mum puts treats in and I spin the tubes around and the treats fly out. My sister Daisy just sits and waits for them to fall out while I do all the work
My friends	I love to meet all dogs out on my walks with my dad, although I know all the humans only walk their dogs to come and see me. My human best friend is my mum of course, but then it's granny. She calls me her grandog. I also love the meat man (My mum's dad), he's a butcher and brings us fresh bones. We stay at mum's friends at Galliano's house when mummy and daddy are away. They love us there. Then there are all the new friends who come and stay at our house. There is Humphrey and Holly, Tilly and Odin. Teddy who is our new puppy friend, he is just like a fluffy teddy bear.

My name is Miffy, I am a cocker spaniel and I live in Lowton with my mummy and daddy and my sister Daisy.

I like chewing up tissue paper, playing in muddy puddles, cuddles with mummy,

walkies with daddy; eating things I shouldn't eat, making a mess. Luckily I am too cute for my mummy and daddy to stay angry at!

I was born on an estate in Newport where I spent the 1st few months of my life with my brothers and sisters. The house I lived in had a room for us puppies, with a massive wide screen TV; it also had a big garden with a trampoline and rose bushes in it.

My favourite thing was to play in the garden and to bite the rose bushes, even though it hurt my mouth!

One day a man and lady from Leigh came to visit me and brothers and sisters. When they came into the puppy room, we were all scared at first and hid, but then we saw that they were friendly and we all went running over to say hello.

I jumped up onto the man's lap to say hello, but when I tried to get off, he dropped me on my head! I squealed and ran into the lady's arms. She gave me a big hug, while I gave the man a dirty look! At least it meant that they had to choose me and become my new forever parents.

A few weeks later, they came back to pick me up. They had a box with a gate on the front to put me in. Everything was ok until they put me in the car and began to drive away. I suddenly got very scared (I hadn't been in a car before) and I cried and cried and wailed and sobbed most of the way to my new home!

I settled in quickly in my new home and I even got to like my new daddy, even though he had dropped me on my head! I also discovered that I like to eat and chew things; I have never grown out of this! I have chewed through electric wires (thankfully not plugged in), lots of my mummy's shoes (daddy's shoes aren't as nice), carpet underlay, lino, the plastic ends on venetian blinds, books, cardboard boxes and lots of paper tissues. One time when we were staying with my mummy's dad, I chewed through the wire on his lawn mower and another time I got into his shed and found his fishing stuff. I had a lot of fun pulling little packets of pike hooks out of his tackle and spreading them on the lawn. Apparently this is dangerous and I was very lucky not to hurt myself, but it was a lot of fun at the time!

Another thing I like to do, is to play in the park and have my mummy or daddy throw tennis balls for me to chase. I don't like it if they try to leave before I am ready.

My favourite thing of all, is to play on the beach when we go to the sea. One time when we went to Southport beach, my mummy left me with my sister Daisy and my Daddy and went to the tea van.

When mummy came back, I heard her but I couldn't see her because the beach was so crowded. So I ran off to try and find her. I ran as fast as I could, but I couldn't see her anywhere, so I ran faster up to the top of the beach and onto the pavement. Behind me, my Daddy was chasing me (I think he thought I was going to run into the road). Mummy wasn't on the pavement, so I ran back onto the beach and up to the tea van. I looked in the back, but mummy wasn't in there either, so ran further down the beach and then there she was in front of me, so I ran as fast as I could and jumped into mummy's arms!

I like to steal and eat food, I shouldn't because it makes me feel ill! I have found and eaten chocolate coins, Danish pastries (they were for my daddy's birthday), I have stolen sausages off my Daddy's plate and a corned beef sandwich when he wasn't looking! But the best one was, when I found a big bag of flour. I talked my sister Daisy into helping me rip it open. It went all over the carpet, so we tried to clean it up by licking it up, but the flour got wet and sticky and then it dried hard and set like concrete, then mummy and daddy came home. They didn't like the mess, but they did laugh (a lot) at me and Daisy covered in flour! Unluckily the flour also made me very poorly sick!

My name is Lillie, I live in Fort Wayne, Indiana, USA

I love to help my mom unpack the toilet rolls. I sometimes forget myself and pretend they are something I have caught!

I'm great at helping with the cooking!

Name	Lillie
Birthdate	18/06/2012
My Mum and Dad	Christy and Steve
I live in	Fort Wayne, Indiana, United States
My favourite toy	always my newest toy, but I always love my Foxy. I also love my green ball
I sleep	with Mum, Dad and Lucky on the bed
Favourite treat	Liverwurst
Other favourite treat	Egg yolk that mum cooks every morning
Good habits	I love to cuddle and sit on mum or dad's lap
Bad habits	I steal socks and underwear
Other bad habit	I counter surf. This is not exactly a bad habit but I am very shy around people I don't know
Favourite walk	Indian Trails Park
Favourite activity	running with my mum or playing chase with my mum.
My friends	my friend Bella, a golden Doodle. Casey and Lucy, Airedale Terriers. Beau and Bella, Labrador Retrievers. Sofie a Beagle, Roxy a Golden Retriever

Hello, I am Miss Lilian but everyone calls me Lillie. Sometimes my mom calls me Girlie-Girl or Pretty Princess.

I am a tri colour English springer spaniel. I am two years old and was born in Fort Wayne, Indiana at Meggison Kennels.

When my mom and dad came to the kennels to pick a puppy, they brought Lucky along with them too. I really liked Lucky so I was happy that I got to go home with them. We bonded right away. Mom and Dad said that I am their third springer and the first girl dog that they have owned, so that makes me very special.

I am a shy girl. I absolutely LOVE my family, but sometimes I am afraid of people that I don't know very well. When I meet new people I like to stay as close to my mom or dad as possible, because I know they will protect me. Mom calls me a Velcro Dog. I'm not sure what that means.

I love to play. My favourite game is chase. Either I chase mom or dad OR they chase me!! Sometimes we run around the yard and sometimes we run around the house. It's fun either way. I usually like to carry a toy in my mouth while I'm being chased. I am pretty fast so they can't catch me.

I'm a good helper, I like trying to help my mom unload big packages of toilet paper; and I love helping with the cooking. I found a cantaloupe melon rind and helped get that out of the way. Always helping out, I am! Mom calls me a Mischief-Girl when I try to help. I think that means I am a good girl.

I am a happy girlie and really LOVE my family, my friends, my neighbourhood, my toys and life in general.

It ROCKS being a springer spaniel.

My name is Lucky, I live in Fort Wayne, Indiana, USA

My Mom and Dad say that I am a 'Love-Dog'

Name	Lucky
Birthdate	Unknown, my mum found me as a stray when I was about 6-8 months
My Mum and Dad	Christy and Steve
I live in	Fort Wayne, Indiana, United States
My favourite toy	a raw hide bone - which I like to hide in the yard
I sleep	with mum, dad and Lillie on the bed
Favourite treat	I like any treat, I'm not picky
Other favourite treat	Egg yolk that mum cooks every morning
Good habits	I don't do potty in the house and I usually stay in my yard
Bad habits	I scavenge for food and things to chew when mum and dad are away
Other bad habit	I eat Lillie's food when she is not looking
Favourite walk	I am old and really can't walk very far now, but I used to like to walk in the woods
Favourite activity	Napping
My friends	My friend Bella, a golden Doodle. Casey and Lucy, Airedale Terriers. Beau and Bella, Labrador Retrievers. Sofie a Beagle, Roxy a Golden Retriever

My name is Lucky Charm; sometimes, my family and friends call me Charmer because I am - well, such a charmer!

I'm a Cocker Spaniel, probably mixed with another breed, but I'm not sure what because my Mom found me running along a busy road in 2003. Mom and Dad say that I am a Love-Dog.

My mom was driving home one evening and saw me running around the entrance to an apartment complex. She was worried that I would get hit by a car, so she turned around and came back to try to save me. Honestly, I was worried that a car would hit me too. They were going so fast and I was so young and scared.

My mom came back, but by that time I had crossed the street. So, she got out of her car and tried to catch me. I was afraid of her at the time, as I didn't know if she was going to hurt me or help, so I kept running away. Finally, she caught me! But, when she picked me up I was so scared, I peed on her shirt! She didn't seem to mind though. She brought me home, put me down on the kitchen floor, and I ran over to the couch and jumped on my dad to introduce myself. I was in pretty bad shape, skinny, infested with fleas and ticks, and homeless, but they took me in and took good care of me.

My mom says that she and dad tried to locate my original owners, but no one answered the ads so I got to stay!! I was so happy; I had finally found my forever home!

My new brother, Oreo, was happy too. He was lonely and glad to get a new brother. Oreo was a black and white English springer spaniel. We were best buddies and loved hanging out together. He was a therapy dog. I thought I wanted to do that too, so Mom took me to class, but I failed my final exam. I was still kind of protective of my mom, so I wasn't too friendly to the other dogs, so I didn't pass. I am friendlier with other dogs now though.

Oreo died of Cancer in 2012. I was so sad and lonely after he was gone. We had been together since I arrived, so I really missed him. About six months after he died Mom and Dad decided I needed a new companion, so they got Lillie. I have to admit, she was kind of a pain in the neck when she first came home. She had loads of energy and just wanted to play, play and play!! She didn't understand that I was old and didn't want to play all day! I had to correct her a few times, to remind her of that. But, she has grown on me, and I guess that I do love her.

I am old now, but I can still get into some mischief. Last year I was nosing around the house while Mom and Dad were gone, looking for something to eat and I found an ink cartridge upstairs. Mom wasn't too happy about the ink stain on the carpet. Then, a couple of days after that, I found a bag of dark chocolate chips in the pantry, so I ate them!! YUM!!! I understand that dark chocolate is bad for dogs but it didn't bother me one bit. I guess I'm "Lucky" in more ways than one!!

Life has been good for a stray dog that found a loving home. I wouldn't change one thing.

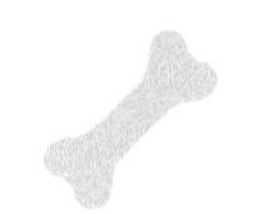

My name is Ronnie, I live in South Yorkshire, UK

I was the runt of the litter and what I lack in size, I make up for in personality!

Name	Ronnie
Birthdate	14/09/2007
My Mum	Nicki
I live in	Barnsley, South Yorkshire
My favourite toy	Rubber balls
I sleep	at every angle possible in bed with my Mum
Favourite treat	Tuna
Other favourite treat	Ginger Biscuits, but unfortunately I don't get anywhere near as many as my human brother Luke
Good habits	I like my daily dentastick to keep my teeth clean. I love a good snuggle whatever time of day.
Bad habits	I like to roll in horse muck and dead things that smell yummy to me, but my mummy doesn't seem to feel the same, so she insists on putting me in the bath, which I always try to escape from.
Other bad habits	I steal Mum's socks and hide them in the garden.
Favourite walk	my favourite walk is at our local lake, because I like to bark at the ducks, try to catch the fish and roll in any dead things I can find on the way round.
Favourite activity	playing with my ball, I'm really good at catching it and march round very proud when I catch it without it bouncing. Cuddles come a close second, I am a very affectionate little man.
My friends	after my Mum, my favourite friends are my brother Luke and my Grandma. I didn't really like other dogs because of a naughty doggy attacking me when I was little, but my Mum forced upon me a fury sister, Bella, who is a 9 month old Springer Spaniel. I didn't like her very much at first but Mum said I had to get to get over it, because we rescued her from a very bad place, so now I've stopped being grumpy and I quite like her (but don't tell her that). Even though she has grown much bigger than me, I'm enjoying being like a proper dog, running, chasing and playing with her. Since we got Bella, I also quite like to make friends with other dogs on our walks, because I've realised not every dog wants to hurt me.

Hello! I'm Ronnie the Cocker Spaniel. I'm 7 years old and I've lived with my Mum and human brother Luke since I was 6 weeks old.

I was the runt of the litter and what I lack in size, I make up for in personality. I've been a bit of a pampered boy and I do like to try it on, to push for top dog by pinching my mum's chair or getting in her side of the bed, but I never manage to stay there for long. My life dream is to one day own her space.

I was a bit of a scallywag as a pup, I chewed everything from the kitchen vinyl floor, to Mum's expensive shoes. I even have on the list twenty pound notes, a very expensive dress and a beanbag that made the house look like a snow scene… I thought it looked nice, but Mum didn't seem to agree.

I love going for walks, I love all the smells, chasing birds and catching my ball. As much as I love being out, I'm also a very affectionate dog that loves getting snuggled up for Mummy cuddles. I sometimes make mourny noises, so that I get to sit on Mum's knee; it works like a treat every time.

Up until a few months ago I was an only fur child, but my Mum came across another dog that needed a loving home. I was not very happy about this, despite Mum telling me it would do me good, I took to my bedroom for a good 24 hours, to show my disgust, but then curiosity got the better of me. So I decided I'd give her a chance, went to show the new kid who was boss. It took a few weeks, but now I love my sister Bella. She can be a little bit giddy and because she's now a lot bigger than me, I can get knocked about a bit by her and she tries pinching all my things, but I give her what for and she is learning to follow my rules. My Mum makes sure I get mummy cuddles on my own too and they make me very happy and I don't mind Bella as much when I've had a bit of time to myself.

I love my dog life and I love my family. I get up each day with the same excitement because I know it's going to be another fun filled day.

My name is Scout, I live in Exeter, UK

I am a very clever girl who learns tricks fast

Name	Scout (Girl Scout not Boy Scout!) I got my name from one of mum's favourite books - To Kill a Mockingbird. In it there's a little girl who loves to run about and play and get dirty just like me!
Birthdate	02/08/2010
My Mum	Sandra
I live in	Newton Abbot, near Exeter in the UK
My favourite toy	my Kong Wooba, although I also love to train with my working dummies!
I sleep	in my bedroom (mum sets it up every evening and puts my bed in it). This is so Grandma won't trip over me in the night
Favourite treat	Chips! And anything!!
Other favourite treat	my special dental biscuits
Good habits	I am a very clever girl, who learns tricks fast
Bad habits	I steal jump on Grandma when she least expects it
Other bad habits	when we go to chase the birdies (pheasants), I get so excited I don't always come back when mum uses her whistle and she has to shout, although this year she has started bringing a pocket full of my dental biscuits, so I have been very good, so long as she remembers them!
Favourite walk	anywhere we go that lasts a very long time (has to be over an hour or I cry with disappointment)
Favourite activity	going with mum to find the birdies (pheasants) during the cold time and chasing dummies in the warm time - I even won some prizes last year!
My friends	when mum has to work, I go with Auntie Eleanor and her collies for the day, we go for walkies and we also play agility. But when the weather gets cold (October to February) I go every Saturday and chase the birdies (pheasants) with a whole gang of spaniels! We all have a fabulous time but when I come home, I flop in my bed and don't move till dinner! It's hard work but I love it!!

Hi All! My name is Scout (Girl Scout not Boy Scout). Mum chose my name from her favourite book - To Kill a Mockingbird, the character is a little tomboy just like me!

Mum always wanted a dog. When a friend sent a text with a cute springer puppy she knew, she had to have one too. But right at that moment, she and Grandma were having the house decorated – hardly the best time to get a pup! But she was determined and called the chap the puppy came from, explaining the rotten luck of the decoration and puppy colliding. He let her know more pups were due later in the year and to call then, and you know, that's what she did.

With Grandma they came to the house, spent a long time choosing, but in the end agreed that I was the cutest bundle that they ever did see. Grandma will tell all that she did not remember actually agreeing to having a dog in the house, but as mum rightly points out it was Grandma who pulled the deposit money from HER purse and paid!

When I was just about a year old, mum decided that she and I would learn what a gun dog actually did, so she found a lovely syndicate shoot looking for new recruits – explaining that we knew absolutely nothing about such activities, they cheerfully said just come along you'll both pick it up very quickly. And they were right, although I reckon that I picked it up faster than mum. The head beater – my Uncle Peter will tell all about the amazing retrieve I made in that first year, nearly four years on, it was that good! He and mum were walking along after one of the drives, me happily trotting ahead, when suddenly I stopped! Nose down I started to dig right by their feet and to their amazement, I then dragged a downed pheasant from under the fern they were about to stand on! Well, Uncle Peter looked at mum and with a huge smile said "that is a fabulous dog". Don't I just know it! So talented and beautiful. Modest too!

When we are not at the shoot, mum has discovered the sport of scurry. Me retrieving dummies and being timed, and you bet that I am superb at that too, even got some red rosettes on the mantle as proof!

My name is Ellie, I live in Essex, UK

I am the number one drama queen in our household!

Hi, my name is Ellie and my family are my world. My mummy says I am her everything and I idolise her.

Let's start off by saying I am the number one drama queen in our household and I will do whatever it takes to get attention, from stealing shoes, tea towels and everything else visible and I love nothing more than jumping on mummy's fresh bed sheets with muddy paws!

My favourite thing is going on long walks or on a car ride, I know exactly when this is happening, because daddy puts his special walking coat on and, as I fly around the house wagging furiously, I get under everyone's feet. I wait on the stairs for my lead to be put on and off we go! Norfolk is my favourite holiday and the beach there is amazing- I love the sand between my paws as I run as fast as my little legs can take me.

Back home, I get called to my cushion and I know it's time for me and daddy's daily game of 'growl ups', where I talk to daddy, whilst he plays fights with me, it's my best game ever.

I steal shoes when people take them off, however I am a good girl, as I don't chew them, just leave slobber on them. They think this is bad, because no one can find their other shoe before work, but I think it's highly hilarious!

I do not leave my mummy's side and I let her know when her phone is going off, or a text message arrives by whining. When she's at work, I know when she gets home, as I can hear her car, so I collect my Smiley and greet her at the door with it.

I love my life at my home and I wouldn't want to be anywhere else- besides who will give me bits of custard creams in the morning?

My name is Pepper and I live in St Leonards on Sea, East Sussex, UK

I love Auntie Maggie (Boxer) because I like to play 'catch her tongue' - it falls out of her mouth A LOT!!!

Name	Pepper
Birthdate	01/03/2014
My Mum and Dad	Paula and Paul
I live in	St Leonards on Sea, near Hastings, East Sussex
My favourite toy	Nerf ball launcher
I sleep	with my mum and dad on their bed, snuggled between them
Favourite treat	Liver cake. My sister Mango said it was great & she's right!
Other favourite treat	Cheese
Good habits	I sit still in the shower and get washed to look all pretty. I like to wear my drying coat because it's cosy.
Bad habits	I get excited and head-butt mummy in the face
Other bad habits	sometimes I stand on the table & windowsill, so that I can see out the big front window.
Favourite walk	anywhere new. I like new sniffs & meeting other pooches
Favourite activity	getting a Human to play with my Nerf launcher in the garden
My friends	I have been lucky enough to go to work with mummy before and she works with really nice people who give me lots of cuddles and fuss. I also love Auntie Maggie (Boxer) because I like to play catch her tongue. (It falls out of her mouth lots!)

I am nick-named "shark-face" because I run around with my mouth open showing off my pearly whites!

My name is Pepper and I was born on the First of March. I went to live with my Mum and Dad when I was 14 weeks old.

Apparently my mum thinks that I have hundreds of 'naughty spots'! I would prefer to call them my 'beauty spots'!

My mum can always tell when I am tired, because my eye goes pink. This is easy to spot because one of my eyes is surrounded by white fur & eyelashes.

I can be very vocal and I like to say "no" quite frequently. I think I sound quite assertive, but my mum would say my 'No' sounds more like a whiny Noo. Not

the sound I was hoping for!!

I have just learnt to swim and I love it. When we went to the beach, I thought I would try splashing around in the waves. One of them did catch me unawares and I went under the water for a short time. My mum started to panic a bit. I think she thought she was going to have to come swimming with me and pull me out. But I was fine; I splashed my front paws and legs around a bit and started to swim. I certainly didn't want rescuing; in fact I went back in for some more fun in the waves. It was great fun and I wasn't scared at all.

I love play fighting with Mango. The best game is when I do forward rolls over her. This will get her going and we end up having a good play fight.

I love to learn new things and of course, it's wonderful when I get lots of praise and cuddles.

I love to wrap myself round my mum's neck like a spotty scarf!!

My name is Mango, I live in St Leonards on Sea, East Sussex, UK

If Mummy and Daddy don't put my lead on fast enough, I nibble their bottoms!!

Name	Mango
Birthdate	17/05/2009
My Mum and Dad	Paula and Paul
I live in	St Leonards on Sea, near Hastings, East Sussex
My favourite toy	my green ball with a rope through it
I sleep	With my mum and dad on their bed, or with my human brothers room
Favourite treat	Liver cake. My first mummy gave my new mummy the recipe so it tastes right now.
Other favourite treat	Chicken
Good habits	if mummy and daddy want to sit down, I get off the sofa for them
Bad habits	if mum or dad don't put my lead on fast enough when we go out, I nibble their bottoms
Other bad habits	I like to roll in mud or I roll in the sand on the beach after swimming
Favourite walk	the woods near Guestling. Lots of sniffs and muddy puddles to lie in
Favourite activity	playing ruff and tumble with my new little sister in the front room or garden
My friends	I have two little friends called Albie & Millie, who live at a tearoom. I also have Lily, Duke & Maggie (who are Nanny's Boxer dogs), they come over to play sometimes and I think Dukey is very handsome

I love to sit like a Meerkat and have my elbows tickled!

I am a 5 year old springer spaniel, my nick name is Mango Mooey (Moo for short) despite being compared with a MOO cow, everyone thinks I am very pretty. I had a bit of an admirer in Basil, who was rather smitten with me! (he has sadly passed over rainbow bridge)

When we first met, I would steal his ball from him; being a gentleman, he never took it back - he just waited until I got bored or wasn't looking and stole it back.

I have a little sister call Pepper. I try to be a good role model for her and take care of her. It's hard work sometimes and a big responsibility!

I just love to have my elbows tickled. I haven't met a Meerkat but apparently one of my favourite positions is to sit like a Meerkat, it's the best position for my elbow tickles!

I hate going out in the car. I do try and make this known to my mum and dad, but they don't seem to take much notice and think that I am just feeling sorry for myself! Charming!

I love to go swimming in the sea. It's the only time I will actually retrieve a ball. Well it's more fun when the ball is bobbing away on the waves.

I love the garden, whenever anyone visits, I like to take them out there first. If mum or dad leaves the back door open, I like to lie in the middle of the garden watching the birds. It's a great pastime, but I'm not sure if I would catch one if it landed near to me.

My name is Macy, I live in Norfolk, UK

Name	Macy
Birthdate	27/09/2012
My Mum	Jo
I live in	Nr Cromer, Norfolk
My favourite toy	my wack wack (duck) and my bunny
I sleep	in bed with my mum and dad
Favourite treat	cold ham and chicken pieces
Other favourite treat	doggie treats and maltesers (which I know I am definitely not allowed)
Good habits	dental sticks and a regular groom
Bad habits	I like to jump on mums bed when I've been outside in the wet !! I also get too excited when I see my brother Moshi (cat) and sister Tallulan (cat). I like to push my nose under their bellies and toss them in the air.
Other bad habits	I take up all the room in bed!
Favourite walk	every walk.
Favourite activity	going to the beach and swimming in the rock pools!
My friends	I have lots of friends, but mostly I go to Sonny's house (my best cocker friend) to play or he comes to us. We love to steal each other's toys and then, if I don't get my way, I growl at him. Human best friend after mum and dad and my human sisters, is Granddad who always plays with me and torments me. He loves taking me for a walk too.

My name is Macy. When my family came to get me, I was 8 weeks old and the baby of the bunch. I was a big surprise, as mum and dad had kept me a secret from the children. They told them they were going to pick up a new car. I was the best surprise ever and better than any car. On the long journey to my new home, I couldn't help myself and I pooed in the car. The family were not impressed and we had the windows wound right down.

I spent my first month trying to befriend the cats and chewing up the Christmas paper and some of the gifts under the tree. My teeth were so sharp that I ripped to shreds all the toys I was given. I was too little to climb the stairs, but whenever the girls left their cuddly toys lying around, I stole them (they never then asked for them back). Then I discovered the downstairs toilet and the loo roll - say no more.

One night mum got so fed up with me whining in the early hours that she took me upstairs for a cuddle and I've never looked back since. Every night, when I get tired, I try and wait for mum to come with me, but when she's busy watching TV or doing jobs, I take myself up to our bed, pull back the covers, tuck myself in and snuggle off to sleep, tight in the middle of the bed with my very own pillow.

Yes I am one much loved and very spoilt cocker spaniel. Happy days

My name is Winston, I live in Wiltshire, UK

I like to chew up my mum's pants!!

Name	Winston
Birthdate	01/03/2013
My Mum	Sarah
I live in	Market Lavington, Wiltshire
My favourite toy	Cyril the squirrel. I do like toys with stuffing but mum says she's not buying me those anymore as I make a mess within minutes. I thought I was being helpful!
I sleep	with my mum
Favourite treat	I love cold chicken.
Other favourite treat	Sausage!
Good habits	I am very good at snuggling with mummy and very good at finding toys. We always come back home with a ball or a Frisbee even if I don't take one with me!
Bad habits	I'm a little bit naughty and chew up my mum's pants!
Other bad habits	I do tease my friend Frank, by taking his ball and not letting him have it back!
Favourite walk	I love going on walks where there is water. I am happy then. My mum sometimes looks a bit cross if there isn't any water and I find other things that are nice and smelly to roll around in!
My friends	my best friend is Frank, my Nanny's dog. We go out together most days and play. Sometimes we are a bit naughty and don't come back straight away because we are having too much fun. I also like to stay at Nanny's some nights and sleep in front of the fire with Frank. My Nanny said she wanted a grandchild, but she has me instead! I like to go everywhere with my mum as I'm not too keen on being on my own. I sit in the front seat of the car with my seatbelt on and look out of the window. I make lots of friends wherever I go, but I'm not so keen on those little dogs now, as they bite me. After a long day I like to snuggle up on the sofa and have my tummy tickled!

I once turned myself bright green!

My latest adventure involved the contents of a deer's stomach, which smelt absolutely divine and I had no choice, but to have a good roll in as much of it as possible! It was wonderful, but it seemed to turn my lovely liver and white coat into bright green! I didn't mind, but I'm not sure how my mum felt about this! I had had so much fun rolling in this wonderful odour; I decided to disappear into the woods to see what else I could find. It must have been my lucky day because I sprung upon a deer's leg! I was so chuffed with myself, I had to go and parade my trophy in front of my mum and my best friend, a Labrador called Frank (he is my nanny's dog). I think Frank was really jealous of my find, but couldn't get hold of it. I made sure I ran around with it for as long as I could, it was flopping around a lot in my mouth, but I didn't mind. It was a great game. (For me anyway!) I do love to tease Frank.

After my fun and games, we got back to the car and met some nice town folk who don't come across furry deer legs very often. They thought this was a great "Wiltshire moment"!! My little friend Harley appeared with his dad and thought my new play thing was great fun! He obviously wanted to be part of the action and as the leg was now looking a little worse for wear, I thought it would be nice to let Harley play with it for a while.

Meanwhile, my mum and nanny were getting a little tetchy; they didn't seem to like my new body odour, I think I was beginning to smell really horrible by now and they seemed determined to get me home for a shower.

For some reason my mum had to wrap me in a towel because my Nanny wouldn't let me into the boot of her car. I don't think she wanted her car to end up bright green and smelling of deer insides. This was great for me, as I got to sit on my mum's lap. She even wound the window down for me so I could stick my nose out of the window and take in the country air. I have to say, I wasn't amused when we got home, as my mum made me have a shower, once again I smelled nice, which as a country loving spaniel is a horrible smell!

I love walking with my best friend Frank up on Salisbury Plain; I do like to tease Frank by pinching his Frisbee! On this one occasion it had been raining heavily, so there were lots of nice muddy puddles for me to jump in. While I was splashing around in the puddles, I noticed some very odd looking white fluffy things in the field. My mum told me they were called sheep and that

I must leave them alone. So of course, what did I do, completely ignore my mum and went to see if these sheep wanted to play Frisbee with me. I didn't realise that the fence keeping them in the field, was a special electric one! I could hear my mum calling me to come back, but I have this thing called 'selective hearing' and therefore I couldn't hear her and continued on my quest straight into this electric fence... OUCH! This made me drop the Frisbee in the field where the sheep were. My mum came to rescue me but she had a bigger problem on her hands. My nanny wanted the Frisbee back, which had landed in the field where the sheep were, on the other side of the electric fence! My poor mum had to pull herself into some very funny positions, to get through the fence without getting zapped, but she did it and threw the Frisbee for Frank to catch. Unfortunately her aim wasn't the best and it landed in a very deep and very muddy puddle. Nanny decided she would go and get it, but Frank and I had other ideas, a great game would be to dive in first, in front of nanny and she who could get it. Nanny didn't seem too amused, as she got covered in muddy puddle water and somehow a big clump of wet mud had landed in her hair. Frank and I thought it was great that Nanny wanted to join in our game, but mum thought she looked like something from a scene in a film called 'Something about Mary'.

I love my fun and eventful walks with Frank, Mum and Nanny

My name is Dexter, I live in Cheshire, UK

I eat the post and steal my Dad's clean socks

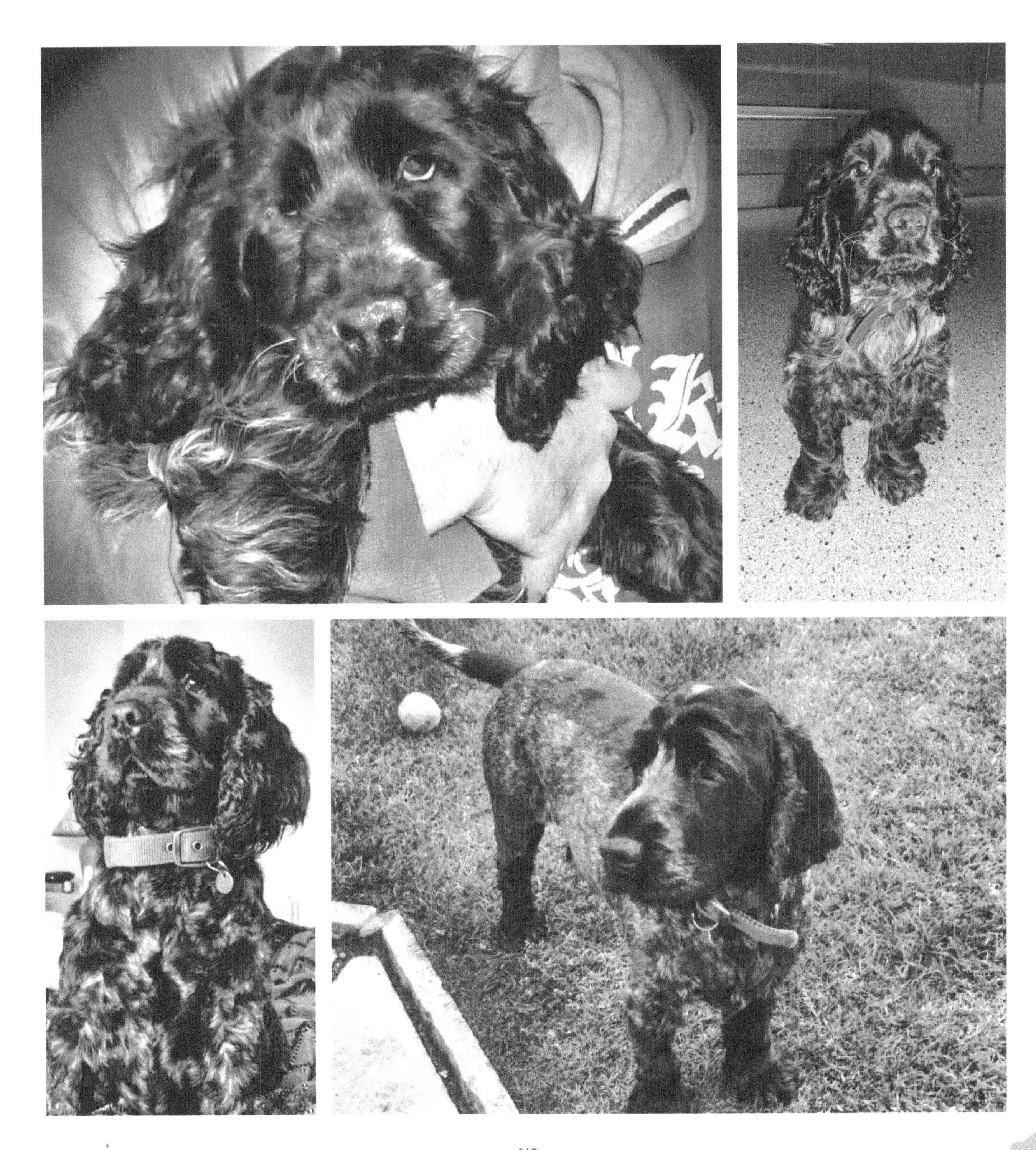

Name	Dexter
Birthdate	04/10/2010
My Mum	Louise
I live in	Cheshire, England
My favourite toy	tennis balls, any soft toy that has a "squeak" in it.
I sleep	in my crate, ever since I was born.
Favourite treat	Fish - Sardine / Mackerel / Tuna
Other favourite treat	cheese. I'm not allowed very much as my Mummy says it's fattening.
Good habits	a dentastick every night before bed. I clean my Dad's ears. I think he likes it.
Bad habits	digging in the garden.
Other bad habits	I eat the post. I steal Dad's clean socks.
Favourite walk	Tytherington woods and the stream that runs through it. Many interesting things to sniff, birds to chase and sticks to fetch.
Favourite activity	My Dad has a car without a roof. I sit on my Mum's knee and we all go out for a ride in the country. I get very excited and love all the lovely smells.
My friends	My Mummy and Daddy and my big brother are my human friends. My best doggie friend is Rosie, a King Charles Spaniel who lives next door to me.

My name is Dexter, or to give me my full name, Delphmount Destiny Dexter. The "Delphmount Destiny" bit is from the breeder, and "Dexter" is the name given to me by my new Mummy and Daddy.

My new Mummy and Daddy collected me when I was eight weeks old. At first, it was scary, leaving my seven brothers and sisters, but very soon I settled into my new home. I was crate trained from birth, so I was very comfortable in my new home with a new crate and toys that had been bought for me.

I quickly grew to love all my new family, or pack, as us dogs would say. But I formed a special bond with my new Daddy, and now, we are inseparable. When I was brought back to my new home in November of 2010, the winter was very cold. Ice and snow was all I saw for the first six weeks! I was very surprised, when one day, when my Mummy took me into the garden, it had changed colour, and it smelled different! Yes, the snow had melted and it was the first time I'd seen green grass! There was me thinking grass was white!

My Mummy and Daddy were keen to "socialise" me in the early days, but as I hadn't had all my vaccinations, my Daddy wrapped me up in a baby's shawl and carried me. It was quite an experience the first time, new sights, sounds and smells for me to get used to. But after a while, it all became quite normal to me.

The early days were very important, as my Mummy and Daddy wanted to take me everywhere with them and wanted me to get used to as many people and places as possible. I even go on holiday with them, which I love.

The house that I live in has a garden that I enjoy playing in. Even more importantly, it is near a wood, which has a stream running through it. Spaniel paradise!

I love going for walks in the woods, lots of very interesting scents to follow and I usually end up going in the water, even on a cold winter's day. When we get home after a walk, if I'm muddy, I have to have a wash before I'm allowed back in the house. I don't understand this, why wash me now, when everyone knows that I will be straight back in the muddy water tomorrow!

My name is Brandi, I live in Liverpool, UK

My back garden is my play area and I love to chase the birds and tease them by not letting them fly off.

Name	Brandi
Birthdate	27/10/2013
My Mum	Jan
I live in	Meols, near Liverpool
My favourite toy	mainly tennis balls but also squeaky snakes
I sleep	upstairs depending on who will have me. Either mum or Martyn
Favourite treat	small pieces of cheese
Other favourite treat	tuna added to my dinner
Good habits	my feed bowl which stops me gobbling my food
Bad habits	I steal socks and underwear at every opportunity
Other bad habits	Paper which I love to pick up including letters. I wake up too early which doesn't go down too well. Jumping up at my humans when they come home but I am just so pleased to see them
Favourite walk	I haven't got one yet as I'm still exploring different ones
Favourite activity	playing with my toys and my humans, mum and Martyn.
My friends	I have two friends, brothers, Brandon who is a cocker spaniel and Barney who is a Cockapoo. We meet up and play in their back garden. I will have a new friend soon called Jake who will be coming to live with us
My human friends	my mum and Martyn. Also my mum's friend Jan who comes in and looks after me whilst mum and Martyn work. She lets me play in the back and takes me for walks, introducing me to new things.

Hi my name is Brandi and I live with my Mum Jan and Martyn in Meols, near Liverpool.

I love meeting other dogs and playing with them, especially my special friend who is Bracken. He is older than me and had an older brother called Bailey but he wasn't very friendly and he scared me as he growled at me. My Mummy explained to me that it was because he was old and was in pain and I had to

be less bouncy around him. That was difficult at first but with Bracken's help I learnt to play with Bailey very gently and I soon began to enjoy my playtime with my friends.

One day though Bracken came to play and there was no Bailey (he had gone over the rainbow bridge) and my friend was very quiet. I couldn't understand what was happening. My Mum and Martyn made a big fuss of Bracken and me and we had a great time just playing quietly in the back garden, both of us getting lots of cuddles which we both loved.

Bracken and I miss Bailey but we still have fun and will have more fantastic playtimes when Barney the new pup is allowed to play too.

I have been taught a lot about playing with other dogs and I understand I have to be careful when I first meet another dog outside, as they might not all be as friendly as Bracken.

I am discovering about the big wide world that is outside my safe place, my home. My mum and family affectionately call me "Pooch" or Pest depending what mood I am in and whether I decide to be my usual go lucky self which is known as hyper!

I get very scared when it comes to new things; I quiver and shake even when a plastic bag is being shaken. Going for walks was a frightening experience as these big things known as Trucks and Buses kept coming towards me. I was expected to carry on walking as if nothing happened. So I sat and wouldn't move.

I enjoy going for walks because when we go out, people stop to make a fuss of me, which I lap up. I am always being told how beautiful and cute I am. Jan, Bracken's Mum, often takes me for walks with Bracken and Barney who is Bracken's new brother, he is great to play with but very barky and I sometimes get scared. He never gives up with the playing but neither do I, especially when it is all four of us because sometimes Jakie (my little brother) comes and plays too.

I have a good life, I have lots of toys to play with, food that I like, the occasional piece of cheese that my Mum spoils me with, and she does spoil me but I love her very much, as I do Martyn, and Bracken's Mum Jan.

I wouldn't change my human Mummy or Martyn and I am very lucky doggie.

My name is Jakie, I live in Liverpool, UK

I chew anything I come into contact with including socks, shoelaces and paper

Name	Jakie
Birthdate	06/10/2014
My Mum	Jan
I live in	Meols, near Liverpool
My favourite toy	I am just getting used to my toys but I really like the rope, even though it's nearly as big as me! I will sometimes share with Brandi but I'm cheeky and will take her toys when she is not looking.
I sleep	in my cage at present but occasionally get cuddles from Mum if I wake up when my teeth hurt.
Favourite treat	all food at the moment. I am on puppy food
Other favourite treat	none at the moment but I can't wait to start trying some
Good habits	being calm when people come to visit. I do then put on my dad eyes as mum and Martyn call them to get people to notice me. I love cuddles and will take as many that are offered and let Brandi share them too
Bad habits	I play with my big sister Brandi and sometimes hurt her then run to my mum or Martyn to be lifted up.
Other bad habits	chewing anything I come into contact with, including socks, shoelaces and paper.
Favourite walk	my back garden at the moment as I am only allowed out there. I will go with Brandi (my big sis) who will show me what to do.
Favourite activity	playing with my toys and my humans, mum and Martyn.
My friends	I don't have any yet but I used to play with my brothers and sisters Mouse, Sydney & Tizzie. Brandi plays with me which is fun. My human best friends are of course my mum and Martyn but also my mum's friend Jan who comes in and looks after me whilst mum and Martyn are at work. She lets me play in the garden and will take me on walks with Brandi when I'm old enough.

My name is Jakie but sometimes I get called Jake

I live with my Mum and Martyn in Meols, near Liverpool.

I have had lots of happy times in the short time I have lived with Mum and Martyn. The first happy time was when I first met them and they came to see me when I was only a little pup. I had cuddles from both of them but didn't really understand who they were then.

They came to visit me a second time and I sat on my Mum's lap, had loads of cuddles whilst my brothers and sisters watched on. Before they left they put me in a blanket and then gave it to my Mum to take away with her and I went back with my brothers and sisters. The humans kept on calling me Jakie or Jake. Sometimes I answered to it but it was very confusing as I already had a name.

The next bit was more confusing as my Mummy Jan came again and I had to say goodbye to where I was living. Mummy Jan carried me out to the car and passed me over to Martyn. I then got a nice surprise as there was another dog in the car who looked at me, growled slightly and turned their back. This scared me so I cuddled up closer to Martyn and waited to see what was going to happen next. We went on a car drive; I had been on short journeys but not one as long as this. Eventually we got to my new home.

We went inside and the other dog came too. I found out that she was my big sister Brandi, who I now follow everywhere, play with and run around in the garden with. That first night, I stayed in the downstairs room, there were thcsc pads on the floor, I got praise when I used them and not told off when I didn't. Everything was very strange and new. I went exploring along with playing with Brandi of course.

Later on my mummy gave me some food which I ate up, then it was bedtime. There was this big object which had my bed in, so I went in and curled up. I didn't go straight to sleep as everything was new. I cried a little bit but fell asleep after a while. I woke up later and didn't know where I was and started to whimper. Mummy Jan came and took me out and gave me cuddles and I fell asleep.

I have great fun with Brandi, meeting lots of different people and doing new things every day.

I love my Mum, Martyn and Brandi and I want to continue to explore, learn new things, play with my toys and friends.

My name is Meg, I live in Lincolnshire, UK

I was rescued and have now lived in my forever home for 18 months.

Name	Meg
Birthdate	Unknown (Rescue) my mum thinks I'm about three
My Mum	Pat Little
I live in	Lincolnshire
My favourite toy	Nylabone
I sleep	in my own bed in mum and dad's room but if dad is working then I sneak into mum's bed
Favourite treat	Wonky chomp.
Good habits	I am a very good girl when I am called and always come back
Bad habits	I eat Fern's poo! Disgusting!
Favourite walk	I love the woods near our house
My friends	my best friends are Fern and Monty the boxer who also shares our home.

I used to live with five other Springer Spaniels but ended up in a Rescue Home

Hi, my name is Meg and I live with my Mum and Dad in Lincolnshire.

I used to live with five other springer spaniels but one day my owner was made homeless and I was taken to a rescue centre in Coningsby, Lincolnshire.

Thankfully my mum helped out with their dog walking and she took pity on me and said I could go and live with them.

I went for a sleepover first to make sure that Fern (Springer) and Monty (boxer) would let me move in with them.

Luckily, we all got on really well and they liked me. I liked them too so now I live in my forever home.

I am different to my sister Fern, I don't like to run after smells, I much prefer to stay close to mum and dad, however if there is any poo to be found I will find it!!. I also hate it when my mum tries to give me warm baths. Why on earth would I want to smell any different than the way I do already.

That was 18 months ago and I love my new home. I get long walks, yummy food and cuddles. What more could a dog wish for!

My name is Fern, I live in Lincolnshire, UK

A few years ago, I found myself in a sticky situation with some Super Glue

Name	Fern
Birthdate	April 2008
My Mum	Pat Little
I live in	Lincolnshire
My favourite toy	my ball
I sleep	I sleep with Meg on our own bed unless Dad is away and then we sneak into mum's bed
Favourite treat	Wonky chomp once a week when mum goes shopping
Good habits	I am a very cuddly dog and will lie all day with you
Bad habits	I sometimes have selective hearing, especially when there are squirrels around
Favourite walk	I love the woods near our house
My friends	my best friends are Meg and Monty the boxer who also shares our home.

A few years ago I got myself into a spot of bother!

I live with my Mum and Dad in Lincolnshire. A few years ago I got myself into a spot of bother!

Mum had left the garage door open and I managed to sneak in without her noticing me. It was great as there were lots of boxes to rummage through. Apparently I have a habit of stealing things!

I found a small tube that seemed interesting so I took it into the garden to investigate further. I was having a good old chew on it when mum came over to see what I was doing. Well, when she saw what I had in my mouth she started acting very odd. She held my mouth open and wouldn't let me close it. She then got Rachel to get a glass of water and started washing my mouth out.

Next thing I was bundled into the car and taken straight to the vets. Mum was telling everyone in the vets what I had done and everyone found it very amusing. After the vet had made a phone call I then found out that apparently super glue isn't toxic!!! To be honest I couldn't see what all the fuss had been about.

I love to run around with my nose pressed to the ground as I am obsessed with smells. I can be quite naughty, as I tend not to listen to mum and dad when they tell me to come back. I never run away, I just have selective hearing because I have such fun.

My other favourite pastime is mud. I just love it, but hate that warm soapy water they bath me in when we get home!

My name is Ollie, I live in Lancashire, UK

I am nicknamed Ollie two balls by my mum's friends!

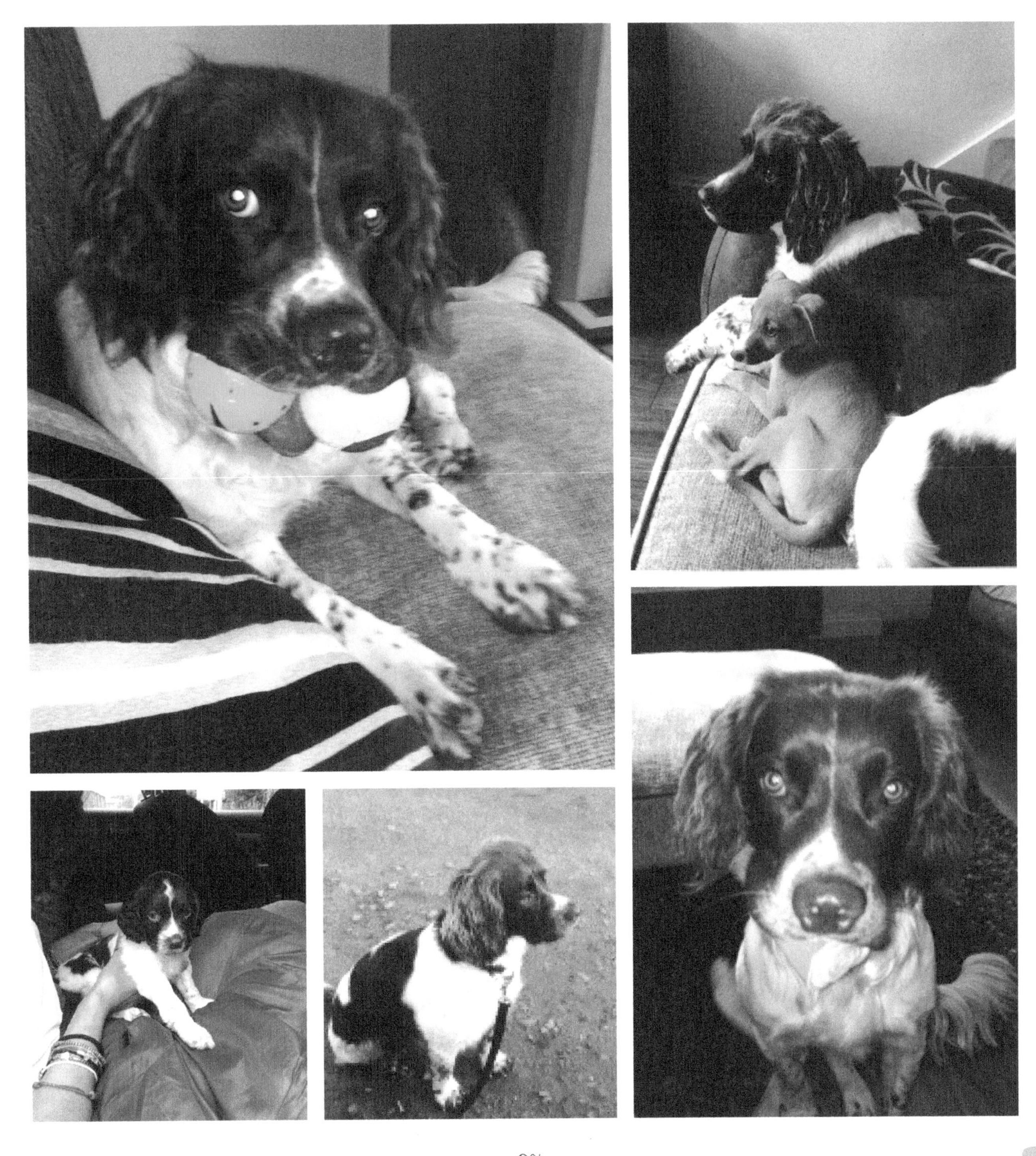

Name	Ollie or if I have been naughty - Oliver (English Springer Spaniel)
Birthdate	27/07/2012
My Mum & Dad	Michelle and Lee Lord
I live in	Littleborough, Lancashire
My favourite toy	any ball and my squeaky toys which have to be replaced frequently, as I chew the squeak out.
Favourite treat	My Mum's roast meats, although I'm quite fond of pigs' ears!
Good habits	giving cuddles, cheering people up with my antics. My claim to fame is carrying two balls in my mouth!
Bad habits	My mum thinks I'm faultless, however, my Dad is always moaning about my toys being left around the house and I do like to pinch the empty toilet roll tube and chew it up!
Favourite walk	I love Wardle Reservoir and Hollingworth Lake. I can run, sniff and swim here. I also like to ramble over the Pennines.
Favourite activity	Hide and seek indoors. Mum hides my toys and treats and I love sniffing and searching for them. Of course my most favourite pastime like all Springers, any activity that involves mud and water!
My friends	I just love my Mum and Dad, they are my best friends and great fun. I do like to play with my new cousin, Maya (Whippet/Beagle) who drives me crazy by chewing my ears.
Travel	I'm a well-travelled Spaniel and have enjoyed Cruising on the Norfolk Broads, Caravanning on Anglesey and this year we toured Scotland, where I swam in the many Lochs and climbed Ben Nevis with my Dad. I have a wonderful life and make my Mum and Dad very happy.

My name is Ollie, I'm an English Springer Spaniel and I'm 2 1/2 years old. I was born in Leigh Lancashire, and was one of an eleven-strong litter! Six of my siblings had already found new homes when my Mum arrived and she fell in love with me instantly!

As a puppy I was particularly fond of testing my new teeth on anything I could, from shoes, slippers and flip-flops to cushions, mail and even the kitchen units!

Thankfully, I've grown out of that stage, although my Mum thought I never would! I now love chasing balls and anybody holding one has my undivided attention! I can catch and carry 2 balls (sometimes even 3) at once and some of Mum's friends have nicknamed me 'Ollie two balls'!

I have a fabulous home life and am rarely bored! My Mum plays hide-and-seek with me, where she hides toys and treats around the house for me to find! I love going on long walks with my Mum and Dad around our local area, Wardle Reservoir, Hollingworth Lake and the Pennines are my favourite places (especially for swimming). I like to travel by car and love having my head out of the window with my ears flapping. I often see people smiling and pointing as I pass by! Another of my favourite places is The Red Lion pub (Mum and Dad's local), everyone seems to know me and the landlord always has treats at the ready!

I have been to some wonderful places with Mum and Dad! We've sailed on the Norfolk Broads, caravanned on Anglesey, stayed in a log cabin in Yorkshire and toured Scotland in a campervan, I even conquered Ben Nevis with Dad! This year we will be seeing the Lake District and Wales, where I will be adding more mountain climbs to my list!

I have a very nutritious diet and am as healthy as I look! I eat mostly raw meat but have that supplemented with a personalised kibble mix, steamed veggies and other meat treats.

I absolutely love my life and the people in it (Grandma always makes a fuss of me), it's a Springer's life, WOOF!

My name is Poppy, I live in Kent, UK

I love to chase the squirrels in my garden but haven't caught one yet!

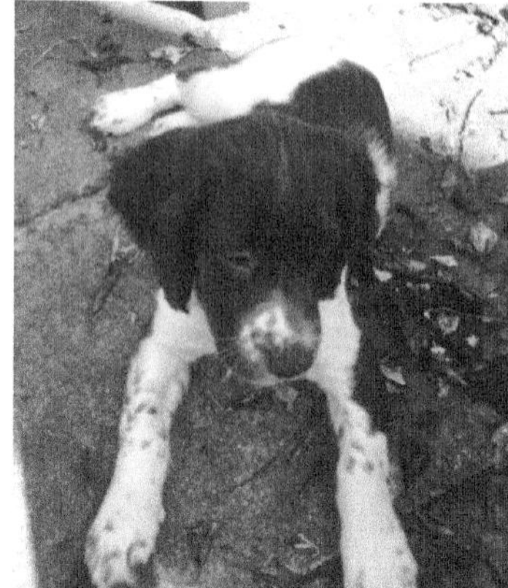

Name	Poppy
Birthdate	03/03/2011
My Mum	Diane
I live in	Walmer, Kent
My favourite toy	I love balls and my Father Christmas soft toy.
I sleep	wherever I want to
Favourite treat	any treat is my favourite treat
Other favourite treat	Chicken skin and gravy
Good habits	I don't bark a lot
Bad habits	I don't really have any bad habits
Favourite walk	walking along the seafront from Walmer to Kingsdown or Walmer to Deal and going for a swim in the sea
Favourite activity	playing ball and trying to catch the squirrels in the garden.
My friends	I regularly meet with Maise and Augusta, 2 labradors. Tia the ESS, Gizzi the Pomeranian and sometimes Stella the German Shepherd, she is still a puppy and tries to eat my head a lot, which I don't like!

My name is Poppy and I live with my family Diane, Paul and Charlotte in Walmer, Kent, and I was born on the 03/03/2011.

I was chosen by my family because when they came to visit me I pulled a plant from a container and ran around the garden with it in my mouth, which they thought was very funny! I am called Poppy because my previous owner didn't give any of us names and just called us puppy which I responded to very well so they decided to call me Poppy which is very similar to puppy.

We live near the beach and I love to go for a swim in the sea and go for walks in the countryside which is also near to where I live.

I love playing ball, and when I go into the living room I have to empty my toy box of all my toys, Mum says I am worse than a child! I also love to chase the squirrels in the garden, but I never catch them.

I have some lovely doggy friends called Maisie and Augusta (Labradors),

Tia (Springer Spaniel) and Gizzi (Pomeranian). I also have a friend called Stella (White German Shepherd) but she likes to bite my head which I don't like and usually have to give her a nip for her to leave me alone.

I have a very happy life and know that I am loved very much.

My name is Hermann, I live in Dartford

When I'm in my favourite woods my tail whirls round like a windmill.

Name	Hermann
Birthdate	16/09/2008
My Dad	Dave
I live in	Dartmoor, Devon
My favourite toy	My Badger
I sleep	with Dave on 'my' bed
Favourite treat	Roast pork crackling, fresh from the oven
Other favourite treat	Ice Cream!
Good habits	I never stray far away from whoever is looking after me. Unless there is water nearby, or pheasants I only bark at strangers coming into the house, and never fight. I can lie in for hours.
Bad habits	I unpair socks, effortlessly.
Other bad habits	I've been known to chase - and catch - the odd pheasant (only pheasant, nothing else)
Favourite walk	anywhere where there is undergrowth and water. Woodland with algae-covered oak is my top habitat. Ideally with a river running through it. And beaches too - any season thanks.
Favourite activity	apart from walking and swimming. Hide and seek with my Badger, with roast pork cracking as the reward - that is pretty much my heaven.
My friends	I live with a Collie girl called Kes, who is only one and even more ball-y than me. She uses her eyes and I use my nose more, but otherwise we are pretty well matched - she's quiet and gentle. WE make a great team on walks. I spend a bit of time with my cousin Mattie, who is a small Schnauzer. She's a tearaway. We're a bit like Lady and the Tramp, but in reverse. Oh, and Fred the old, old and tall, tall Deerhound whom I have just met and who has - at the age of 6 - taught me to cock my leg. Oh and Bertie, my French Bassett friend - we always spend Christmas together and share quite a lot of turkey with each other.

I am six years old, a black working cocker who has moved from London to Devon. My favourite habitat of all, beyond the beach, meadows, moor and cities (ugh!) is the woods. Not the dark, lifeless pine forests where I pick up hundreds of little sticks that tangle my feathers and give Dad yet another me-related job to do in the evening. No, the deciduous ones – oak, beech, birch, ash – with moss growing on their special green branches and just the right undergrowth for a working cocker to live his life in.

Even better if there's a river running through it, like the Teign. That's when you'll see me on top form, tail twirling in maximum windmill mode, nose to the ground galloping forward. If there's a ball to find, or rabbits around, there's no other place I'd rather be. It's where I learned to perfect my cocker bounce, sometimes 8 or 9 of them in a row, my specially designed ears help lift me up like wings.

My perfect day is hours of bouncing, whatever the weather, and then the trot home with dinner (hot beef stew I hope) on my mind. A day like today in fact, now with the fire going and daylight nearly spent, I'm about to turn turtle with my head to one side and snooze next to Dad, who now has all sorts of things to waste his time doing.

Funny thing he is. But my dad is my everything and I love him more than cheese.

My name is Jessie, I live in South Wales, UK

I love to roll my ball backwards and forwards ALL Day and ALL Night!

Name	Jessie
Birthdate	17/07/2010
My Parents	Lyanne and Kelpy (real name Richard)
I live in	South Wales, United Kingdom
My favourite toy	Tennis Balls
I sleep	on the sofa
Favourite treat	Cheese.
Other favourite treat	Carrots, I get these after my evening meal.
Good habits	I am very obedient, I do whatever my mummy and daddy tell me
Bad habits	I tell Woody, my brother, off all the time and I'm quite mean to him. I don't let him anywhere near mummy and daddy's things.
Other bad habits	I sneak upstairs when mummy and daddy open the baby gate but they don't seem to mind as I'm such a good girl.
Favourite walk	I love to run in the long grass so any big field.
Favourite activity	rolling my ball back and forth to my mummy and daddy. I do it ALL day and ALL night!
My friends	I live with Woody, but he's a really really naughty boy. I have to tell him off all the time. I let mummy and daddy know when he has been naughty and then help them tell him off. I don't have any friends, I don't really like other furry friends. As long as I have my tennis ball and my mummy and daddy, I am really happy.

My name is Woody and I live in South Wales, UK

I love to steal socks and swallow them whole!!

Name	Woody
Birthdate	12/05/2009
My Parents	Lyanne and Kelpy (real name Richard)
I live in	South Wales, United Kingdom
My favourite toy	anything that isn't mine
I sleep	on the big sofa.
Favourite treat	Cheese, I love cheese!
Other favourite treat	Carrots, I get these after my evening meal.
Good habits	I give the best cwthes (cuddles)
Bad habits	I steal socks, tea towels, Jessie's toys
Other bad habits	I like to hump Jessie's bed but mummy and daddy don't like me doing this.
Favourite walk	anywhere I can run free
Favourite activity	I love going to our caravan, so much fresh air and so many people to see
My friends	I live with Jessie but we don't really get on very well. She is quite mean to me. She growls at me all the time, even when I just walk past her. I don't have any best friends but I love meeting all furry friends. I get so excited when I see a fellow friend. I run up to them and chase them. I love all humans; they give me so many tickles. They all say how cute I am. But I know this already!

We are Woody and Jessie from South Wales, UK

Our mummy had a furbaby before us called Dylan but he was a Yorkshire terrier. He left for Rainbow Bridge and Mummy was really upset and said she never wanted another furbaby because it was too hard saying goodbye. That was until she saw me, Woody. She fell in love with the picture of me and couldn't wait to come and visit me with my fur mummy and fur brothers and sisters. She drove a long way to come and see me and we fell in love immediately. I couldn't wait to go and live with them. They came back to pick me up two weeks later and we had a long journey home. I sat on mummy's lap

all the way home and I was a really good boy and never wee weed on her at all. When it got dark they put me in a really big cage with all these furry things, but they didn't move like me. I didn't mind and slept all night. I didn't cry once. Mummy and Daddy were so proud of me.

When I was 16 months old daddy wanted another furbaby. Mummy wasn't too keen on that idea though. We were on holiday in our caravan and they drove for a long long time to go and see another furbaby. They flipped a coin to decide whether they would have another and daddy won. Mummy cried all the way home and I had to give her lots of licks to make her happy.

When Jessie came home I was so happy, I had a new playmate. She was so little but I loved having someone to play with. She became very grumpy though and started to be really mean to me. She growls at me all the time. She tells Mummy and Daddy whenever I do something I shouldn't do.

I love to steal socks and swallow them whole. I know I'm a naughty boy but I do like being naughty as they don't stay cross with me for long because I'm so adorable.

Jessie is always good, she never does anything wrong. Well she did once! She ate mummy's new leather sofa TWICE. I got the blame because I ate all the bits of leather to try and cover up for her, but they realised it was her when she destroyed her bed. She doesn't do it anymore though. All she is interested in is her tennis balls and she doesn't like it when I pinch them.

We love going down to our caravan and we both get so excited when get to the lane. We both bark and cry until daddy lets us out and walks us up the lane. I'm very naughty when we go there through. I wake mummy and daddy up all the time to feed me throughout the night. They never give in though.

Both Jessie and I love our mummy and Daddy but only like each other - JUST!

My name is Liliuokalani, I live in London

My mum is from Hawaii!! That's how I got my name.

Name	Liliuokalani
Birthdate	2012
My Mum	is from Hawaii!! That's how I got my name.
I live in	London.
My favourite toy	My Frisbee. I'll do ANYTHING for it. Oh and my mum's used socks.
I sleep	in my kennel. It's my safe place!
Favourite treat	anything that smells terrible to my mum.
Good habits	being the sweetest girl to everyone I meet.
Bad habits	pulling on my lead and making mum's arms hurt!
Favourite walk	any beach where I can run and be my wild self, especially if daddy is running with me. I particularly like beaches where lots of birds hang out.
Favourite activity	chasing my Frisbee and throwing myself into very dirty water.

I was born in Kent with my 2 sisters and 1 brother. When I was 3 weeks old a woman came to see me. She said she had come to find a new family member and she wasn't sure which one of us (me or my siblings) it would be. I was too busy sniffing anything and everything in sight to really notice what was going on, but my siblings were climbing all over the lady anyway, so I didn't think it was worth bothering with.

Well, what do you know? Three weeks later the lady came back with a man and that was the first time I really met the people who were going to be my new mum and dad! Two weeks later they came back to get me (mum sleep walked the night before because she was soooo excited) and I went home with them to my new forever home. Mum even took time off work to just be with me for the first few months. I did all I could to be a good girl, never crying at night and learning to pee outside within a week.

Mum and dad say they cannot imagine their lives without me. And I couldn't agree more!

My name is Otto, I live in Cambridgeshire, UK

Name	Otto
Birthdate	31st October 2012
My Mum	Kimberley
I live in	St Ives, Cambridgeshire, England
My favourite toy	leaves off trees and my blanket
I sleep	in my bed in the dining room
Favourite treat	Bits of dried liver
Other favourite treat	licking out wotsits crisp packets.
Good habits	I always sit on my "spot" on the sofa (the one with the blanket on) and I always sit and wait to be given a treat.
Bad habits	chasing cats and barking at passers by.
Other bad habits	not always coming back when called if I get too excited about what I'm chasing.
Favourite walk	I love going for walks with my Dad at the end of a day's work on the family farm, either round the lake or the spinney, because there's lots of pheasants and bunnies to chase and it's even better when Mum comes too!
Favourite activity	A day spent shooting, either beating with mum or being peg dog with Dad (it's more fun with Mum but shh don't tell Dad I'm at my happiest chasing leaves).
My friends	my mates are Toby, Poppy and Buster, all are Springers like me and live on the farm. I get very excited when I know I'm going to see them but I do like to tease them with their toys and play fight with them but it's ok because they always play back. Humans are my friends too, especially ones that give me treats and lots of belly rubs!

Hi, my name is Otto, I live in St Ives, Cambridgeshire, England with my Mum Kimberley and Dad Martin and two cats Zeus and Theseus, who live upstairs and never want to play with me! I'm 2 years old and still play like a puppy, my favourite toy is my blanket, I love it when Dad plays tug of war with me with it. I have a bone which I like to carry round with me, just to show off that it's mine. I love running around chasing leaves, rabbits and pheasants, it's so much fun!

I haven't always been able to run around though, a year and a half ago I was on a walk with my Dad running around, excitedly smelling all the smells and chasing bunnies, when my front leg went all funny, I screamed in pain, and my Dad came running, he picked me up and my leg just hung at an odd angle, it hurt, it so bad! Dad took me to see other humans who poked and prodded me and wrapped up my poorly leg, they gave me medicine which made me sleepy and then when I woke up Dad had gone. I was scared. When Mum and Dad came to get me then next day I was so excited but I was still in pain. A human told Mum and Dad that I had dislocated and fractured my elbow and that I had to go Cambridge University vet school to have an operation. I rode in the car sitting on Mum's lap, she gave me lots of cuddles but I was scared and in pain so I whimpered a lot. When we got to the vet school I forgot about the pain because it was exciting to be somewhere new and I got to meet new humans. But soon Mum and Dad had to say goodbye to me and I was given more medicine that made me sleepy.

When I woke up I had my leg all bandaged up and I couldn't move very well. Mum and Dad came to pick me up and I was so happy to see them. The vet person told them that the accident had happened because of a genetic condition called Incomplete Ossification of the Humeral Condyle (IOHC), it means that the elbow joint doesn't fuse properly and can break at any time. Spaniels especially suffer from this. And that I'd had my leg screwed, pinned and plated. They were told I would have to be on complete cage rest for 6 weeks, I didn't like the sound of that and neither did Mum and Dad!

Cage rest is no fun, I wasn't allowed to go on walks or run around even when I started to feel better and although I got taken outside to go to the toilet I wasn't allowed to stay out and play. I got clever though, I used to spend 10 minutes sniffing around and trying to find a good place to go! If I was good in the evenings I was allowed to sit with Dad on my spot on the sofa for cuddles but if I tried to get down I had to go back in my cage.

I started to feel better and wanted to go out and play very quickly but soon had to go back to see the nice people at the vet school. They gave me some sleepy medicine again and took a picture of my other elbow. Bad news; I had a fissure in the other elbow too, so Mum and Dad got the vet people to pin it preventatively so no more breakages running around, but the bad news was I had to be on another 6 weeks' cage rest. I was a good boy though and did as I

was told, most of the time. My legs are all better now and I like to run around all the time. Mum and Dad were told I probably shouldn't be too active but there's no stopping me, I'm a Springer, I'm going to do what I do!

My Dad is a farmer so I go to work every day with him. I love it! I get to ride in tractors and diggers, chase straw, play in mud, chase cats, play with my three Springer friends and go for lots of long walks across fields and round the lake. I also get to go on pheasant shoots with Mum and Dad. Mum takes me beating. It's my job to run and spring through the cover to scare the pheasants up into the air. Mum whistles me so I know where she is and I keep running back to her to tell her I'm doing a good job. If Mum doesn't come with us then I have to be peg dog with Dad. It's not as much fun because I have to sit still, I don't like sitting still, but I do get to go catch the pheasant. I'm not good yet at bringing them back to Dad, I think that Dad shot it so he should go get it! Life is good being a farm dog, I think I did well choosing Mum and Dad when they came to get a puppy, I'm having so much fun!

My name is Lucy, I live in Stoke on Trent, UK

I love a Milky Caffeine Free Tea with Lactose Free Milk and toast

Name	Lucy Lockett
Birthdate	01/08/2011 (a rough guess as I am a rescue)
My Mum	Katie
I live in	Stoke on Trent
My favourite toy	Tennis Balls, my yellow kong or my Dad's slippers
I sleep	I sleep in the kitchen with my Brother (Rafferty, a black lab) in a comfy bed with pink fleeces to cover me when it's cold
Favourite treat	Any biscuits, bones, chews or human good that I am allowed (never bananas though as I have gone off them).
Other favourite treat	A Milky Caffeine Free Tea with Lactose Free Milk and toast
Good habits	Having my teeth and ears cleaned and my nails clipped
Bad habits	Stealing shoes and stalking squirrels
Other bad habits	Jumping in the mud and water. Generally anything wet or smelly. Not letting my brother have cuddles, as it's all about me!!
Favourite walk	Anywhere where there is water and with my Grandad John.
Favourite activity	Getting out and about as much as I can. I loved my recent holiday to Sherringham in Norfolk with my Nan and Grandad. I also love shooting with Rafferty and my dad at the weekends.
My friends	My best friend is Rafferty my brother and also Alfie and Bobbin my cat brothers. Then it has to be my Grandad as he adores me and walks me miles and miles with a complimentary blow dry on our return. I have lots of friends when I go on walks nearby. Bella (collie cross) and Stanley (border collie). Generally I love people, dogs and cats but I do feel the need to always chase squirrels!

My Best Friend ...Lucy Lockett Aged Approximately 3 and a bit!

I stumbled across Lucy (who was then called Bramble) by accident when I was looking to rescue a Labrador to help me during a particularly difficult period in my life. After initially having been shown a Springer Spaniel, I walked away having the common misconception that Springers were all a bit crazy! However, this dog stirred something inside me and needless to say Bramble was collected within a week and I promptly renamed her Lucy (my surname is Lockett so I thought it very apt) ready for a new to her new life. Lucy has been a total bundle of joy ever since and I am truly addicted to her and the breed, matching all that I look for in a dog!

Lucy's Background

Well this is a bit of a grey area and if anyone reading this can help then I would be very grateful. As I mentioned earlier whilst looking for another Labrador, a local rescue society told me they had heard about a local farm in Biddulph, Staffordshire that were having to sell up and re-home their breeding bitches (seemed like a puppy farm to me as there were 19 kennelled dogs with a sign outside saying puppies for sale). The Owner told me that she had no "papers" for Bramble (apparently all of her Springers were called this same name hence me changing it quickly). I was told that Lucy had been purchased from a game keeper who had 3 children and could not cope with her so she got her under the false pretences of having her as a pet. This was clearly not the case, luckily for me Lucy had not yet had her first season or I did not think that I would have been allowed to have her. As luck would have it this happened within a week of me having her. It was meant to be and of course she has since been spayed. I suppose it does explain why Lucy settled so quickly and is amazing with children, other dogs and my cats!

It is a shame that I do not have even the smallest bit of information about Lucy, even just to know her birthday would be lovely which I have estimated to be the 1st of August 2011. I contacted the Owner of the farm several times before she moved even offering money but with no success.

On to happier times

Lucy has an amazing life now living with her brother Rafferty a handsome black Labrador enchanting all that she meets with her clever, loving and bubbly personality. I was not expecting there to be such a huge difference in the breed to Labradors and nobody warned me about their love all of wet things! I discovered this the hard way usually when I was running late and had not incorporated time for a dog bath as well as a walk!

Lucy loves swimming, going shooting (she had natural instincts there), playing with a ball, chasing squirrels but equally to be cuddled up on the sofa.

I can quite honestly say that I never want to be without a Springer Spaniel in my life to keep me on my toes and show me such fun and happy times.

My name is Ruby, I live in Cheshire, UK

Stan saved my life a few years ago when I was run over and needed a blood transfusion

Name	Ruby
Birthdate	03/04/2010
My Mum & Dad	Emily and Josh
I live in	Cheshire, England
My favourite toy	I don't really play with toys but I do like teddies.
I sleep	with my mum and Dad in their bedroom, sometimes I sneak onto their bed
Favourite treat	tuna, I love licking the leftovers from the tin
Other favourite treat	Duck, I love to beg (although I know I shouldn't) when mum and dad have it
Good habits	I am very good at standing still while mum washes me with the hose pipe, I don't know why she bothers, I will only be dirty again tomorrow. But I do love a good rub with a nice warm towel afterwards.
Bad habits	I don't think I have any bad habits, although mum doesn't seem too impressed when I lick her face when she's asleep. When I jump on her in the middle of the night.
Other bad habits	sometimes I refuse to jump into the car after my walk. Mum always seems a little bit cross but I'd much rather be on my walk than in the car, and who can blame me.
Favourite walk	the fields down the road from my house. I meet Nanny and her pup Harper (Labrador) there. There are lots of pheasants, rabbits and birds for me to chase.
Favourite activity	Chasing birds and rabbits. I'm so happy when I catch one. It makes a lovely present for mum.

My friends	Everyday my dad's friend's dog Patch (Jack Russell) comes to the farm where I live to play with me while the grown-ups work. We have great fun, she can fit down the rabbit holes and flush them out for me to chase. When mummy gets home from work she takes me for a walk where I meet Harper. She is only a pup and very annoying. However, since she has caught her first rabbit I have grown to love her. At the weekend my dad's other friend Lily (springer) comes to play. And of course, my good old friend Stan. He saved my life a few years ago when I was ran over and needed a blood transfusion.

I spend my days with dad out in the fields - I play, he works!!

My name is Ruby and I live with my Mum and Dad in Cheshire. I used to live outside when I was a puppy, but now my Mum and Dad have turned the barn into a HUGE kennel for me! There are three beds and I just love choosing which one to lie on. I have so many stories I can tell you about all the fun I've had catching rabbits, birds and ducks and embarrassing my Mum.

I think I'm a very lucky dog. I never have to be left home alone because my Dad works at home, well outside! He works on the yard and I'm allowed to run around in the fields all day long and I get really muddy! Sometimes my friend Patch joins me and because she's only little (Jack Russell) she can fit down the rabbit holes and send them out for me to chase. There is a down side to being on the yard though – the cars! We have to be very careful. One sunny day, just after I was two, my Dad came home and I'd just been running in the fields. As it was so hot I decided to lie under my Dad's HUGE van to get out of the sun. I'd only just closed my eyes when the van started moving. I tried to get out but I didn't make it in time. I don't remember much after that, Mum says I was out of it! But apparently they took me to the vets and a special hospital where I was given a blood transfusion. The vet took some blood from my friend Stan to give to me! How cool is that? Anyway I stayed in the vets for four days and I had a broken jaw. I didn't eat for a whole week and when I ate for the first time that bacon was good!! Mum just kept pulling meat out of the fridge and I couldn't stop eating. Mum was so happy; you should've seen her face! My family say I'm tough as old boots but I've definitely learnt the hard way – sleeping under cars is not the best idea!!

Let me tell you about the time I embarrassed my mum! We went for a walk at a lake and woods near to my house. I love it there! I couldn't believe it this one day when I saw a group of ducks, just chilling by the bushes. I ran after them as fast as I could, but they flew over me. To my surprise I managed to leap into the air and catch one! I suppose they don't call us Springers for nothing. I was so proud of this beautiful present for my Mum. So I took it to her, I was about to drop it at her feet when a lady came over (a posh lady whose dogs wore clothes!). She shouted at my Mum, "Has your dog just killed that duck?" My mum didn't know what to say – it was the first time I'd caught anything. So I decided to give the lady my duck, I dropped it at her feet and it flapped its wings and flew off to the lake. The lady squealed and did a very funny dance. My mum just walked off. I think she had a little laugh to herself.

I like to chase all sorts of small animals. If I catch them I don't ever hurt them I just give them to my Mum. They always run away again and I don't know why, I just want to play.

My name is Harley, I live in Suffolk, UK

I love to sit in the front passenger seat where everyone can make a huge fuss of me!

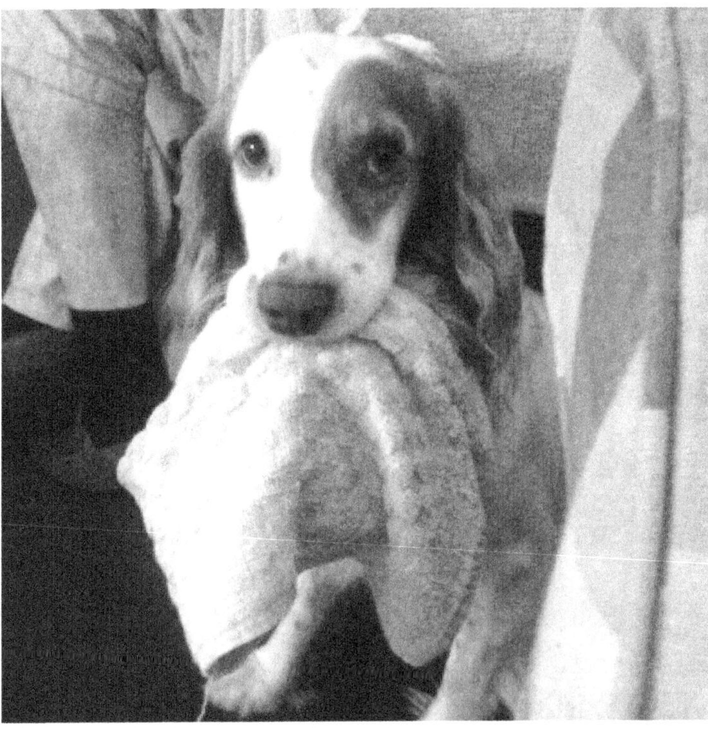

Name	Harley
Birthdate	22/06/11
My Mum	Annie
I live in	Trimly, Suffolk
My favourite toy	I have so many but probably my duck or my bauble ball
I sleep	Mum and dad's bed
Favourite treat	sitting in the front passenger of the car and mum in the back so everyone can see me and make a huge fuss.
Other favourite treat	Every night 9.00pm without fail hide chew stick
Good habits	Err that's a hard one but I love loads of cuddles and quite good at the recall and whistle and I love everybody..
Bad habits	Stealing cushions, shoes, socks etc!!
Other bad habits	Ripping tissues and paper all over the place
Favourite walk	Anywhere, but the field near my house is the best
Favourite activity	going to visit my friend Boo. She has a huge garden and we go crazy in it
My friends	My GSD mum Ellie and girlfriend Boo!

My mum and dad came to rescue me from a home when I was 14 weeks old

After losing our dear golden boy Dodge, the heartbreak and emptiness was unbearable. In our 30yrs together we had never been dog less! At one time, we had five fur babies. All but one lived out happy days with us. (Bandit sadly went missing and we were never able to get him back.)

A friend who is involved with animal rescue, called us when she heard of our loss to tell us of a German Shepherd, 5-6 year old girl who had been abandoned in a barn with another dog. The other had been rehomed so could we help Ellie by giving her a forever home. We went to meet Ellie and needless to say she came home with us. She loved being around other dogs and we still had the cocker bug! So we contacted my rescue lady friend to request that if any cockers came up for rehoming, could she give us a call. Several months later she called to say a young working cocker had come in needing a forever home. My husband hot footed it to the rescue centre where Harley was. It turned out this young dog was in fact 14 weeks old and had been put into the centre at 12 weeks old. Two days later we took Ellie to meet him and it was love at first sight. She fell for him and vice versa! Harley was on his way to his forever home with us. A cocker spaniel and a German shepherd, our favourite dogs, both rescued.

I was intrigued to know why a 14 week old pedigree pup ended up in a rescue centre. Apparently the person who took him in said he was vicious. I was speechless; Harley had shown no signs of aggression. A few weeks later we were out walking in the fields with Harley and Ellie, we met a chap with two young cockers (litter brothers). When the pups met it was just as though they knew each other, playing and running around together. This chap was convinced Harley was from the same litter. We exchanged phone numbers and he gave us the breeder's name. When we got home I checked Harley's vaccination/health check book, the previous owner's name and date of birth. The chap we met earlier in the fields came round with the breeder's address and phone number. When I called her and explained who I was and had given her Harley's details, she was horrified to hear what had happened to Harley. Had she known that the person was not able to keep Harley, she would have willingly given the person back their money and taken back Harley. She did email the person as a follow up puppy check and was told that Harley had gone to a farm because he was a working breed. The Breeder was not happy but overjoyed that Harley was now with us in his forever home. We keep in constant contact and she has sent me copies of Harley's pedigree line. The wonderful thing about this story is that our beloved Blue and Harley are of the same bloodline, so despite being bred hundreds of miles apart they are distant relatives! Perhaps Harley was a parting gift from Blue!

And so the supposedly vicious 14 week old puppy has fallen on his paws!
Loved and spoilt to bits along with his best pal Ellie in their forever home.

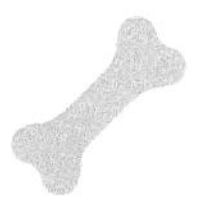

My name is Maddy, I live in West Sussex, UK

I love to chase pigeons, rabbits and Pheasants. I am really good at catching rabbits much to my mum's dismay!

Name	Maddy
Birthdate	14/02/2005
My Mum and Dad	Carol and John
I live in	Horsham, West Sussex
My favourite toy	Always the newest my mum buys me
I sleep	on mum and dad's bed
Favourite treat	Marmalade on toast.
Other favourite treat	Liver bread
Good habits	Keeping guard of the garden each evening
Bad habits	Selective hearing when swimming after ducks
Other bad habits	carrying dead rabbits round with me on the whole walk.
Favourite walk	torch light walks
Favourite activity	Chasing pigeons
My friends	Max the springer, Maki the cocker, Logi the Newfoundland and Mo, a rottweiler cross.

My name is Maddy and I live with my mum and dad in Horsham, West Sussex. I have a wonderful life since I was rescued from my first owners. I am spoilt rotten because my mum and dad love me so much.

I didn't have a very good start in life and my earliest memories are very unhappy.

My first owners didn't really want me and I spent 2 years on my own in a yard, with only pigeons for company. The highlight of the day was when they threw scraps out of the door. Once I tried to go in the door but it was slammed shut into me and it broke my ribs. After this a nice man from the RSPCA came and took me away to a special place called a Spaniel Rescue Home. All the humans were so lovely to me and treated me very gently.

One day my new mum and dad came to pick me up to take me back to my forever home. I had never seen inside a house before so I felt very anxious, especially as it had so many scary doors inside. I was determined not to go anywhere near them in case they hurt me again. Over time and with lots of gentle persuasion from my mum, I came to realise that these were nice doors

and they were nothing to be afraid of.

The other thing I found very scary was this big dark path that seemed to lead up into the sky. My mum told me they were called stairs and that they would not hurt. I took a lot of persuading and lots of bottom pushing from my mum until one day I bit the bullet and just ran straight up them. I had nothing to lose. At the top were the most wonderful soft bouncy things called beds. The best thing was my mum didn't seem to mind me jumping up and sleeping on them. I loved it.

I came to realise all the scary things in the house were ok. I got lots of cuddles from my mum and dad to reassure me which I had never had before.

The best thing ever was something they called 'going out'. It was so big! And full of things to chase! I ran my legs off and kept bashing into trees and fences it was so exciting.

My mum and dad were always taking me to people in white coats called vets to have stitches, they would say 'oh Maddy again' as I bled over the shiny floor.

I am older and well behaved now. My mum and dad hope to find a brother or sister for me and I will get to choose from the rescue centre. I will teach it to chase pigeons, pheasants, rabbits, to run in and out of those doors, bounce on beds and mostly that most humans are nice and will love them unconditionally. Just like my mum and dad.

My name is Tyler and I live in Staffordshire, UK

Name	Tyler
Birthdate	27 May 2011
My mummy & daddy	Lina & Clive
I live in	West Midlands
My favourite toy	All of them
I sleep	With Mummy, Daddy & Olly
Favourite treat	Dentistick
Other favourite treat	Bonios
Bad habits	Barking when Mummy talks to someone when out on our walks
Other bad habits	Pinching people's shoes when they come in
Favourite walk	The woods behind my house
Favourite activity	Playing 'find it' with Mummy and Olly
My friends	We always see Sky the Husky, Max the Patterdale Terrier, Duke the Cocker Spaniel, Bella the Boxer and Jaiger the Cocker Spaniel who looks exactly like me.

Hi people, I'm Tyler and I was born in Staffordshire but moved to the Midlands with my new family.

The day I left home I remember running through some long grass with the lady who looked after me from birth. At the end of the grass were some people who when they saw me scooped me up and showered me with lots of cuddles and kisses. I thought to myself that I quite enjoyed all the attention and that if there was more of this to come then I would be quite happy.

Picture of journey to my new home »

I couldn't believe when I got to my new home how big the garden was and how many new toys I had to play with. I thought 'wow, kisses, cuddles and lots of things to do and to play with'.

My first walk was to a place where there was so much investigating to do and lots of smell around. I learnt that when I heard the words "walkies in the woods" that it meant it was going to be a tiring but very exciting walk.

Life was great living with my new Mummy, Daddy and 2 brothers who showered me with so much love and affection, played lots of games and took me on lots of walks. All was going so well until one day when I was 7 months old my front leg started to hurt. Mummy rubbed it better for me every time I told her, but then there came a time when no matter how much mummy rubbed it, it still hurt. She took me to the doggy hospital and I had to have x-rays to see what the matter was with it. The only way to make it better was to have an operation on it. The day came when I went for my operation. Mummy took me and I had to go in a room without her but with some other people. I don't remember anything after that room except I went very sleepy. When I woke up I found that I had 2 big plasters on my front legs. I don't know what was more embarrassing, the fact that I couldn't stand up properly or that they were leopard print plasters. I thought if any of my friends see me wearing these my street cred is going downhill. I was so pleased when they came off so I didn't feel stupid, but then I had to wear some stupid thing round my head that looked like a lamp shade. My street cred continued to plummet. It felt like ages before I could go for a walk again in the woods, but the day actually came and I ran and ran and ran for ages.

I am now 3 1/2 years old and I thought life couldn't get any better...out on walks every day, playing in the garden with my toys, lots of love and attention from my family...but I was wrong. It goes SO much better.

One day Mummy and Daddy went out one morning and when they came back they had bought a puppy. His name was Olly and he was exactly like me but gold in colour.

As soon as they put him on the floor we moved closer, sniffing and investigating each other. I kind of got the feeling he was going to be here to stay and become my partner in crime. Mummy calls us the 'gruesome twosome' because wherever he goes I follow and whatever I do he copies. But that's fine by me because he's my best buddy and I love him to bits.

Well that's been my life so far and it's been brilliant up to now. The best mummy and daddy in the world, the best brothers and now my best mate Olly. Life just couldn't get any better.

By the edge of a woods, at the foot of a hill,
Is a lush, green meadow where time stands still.
Where the friends of man and woman do run,
When their time on earth is over and done.
For here, between this world and the next,
Is a place where each beloved creature finds rest.
On this golden land, they wait and they play,
Till the Rainbow Bridge they cross over one day.
No more do they suffer, in pain or in sadness,
For here they are whole, their lives filled with gladness.
Their limbs are restored, their health renewed,
Their bodies have healed, with strength imbued.
They romp through the grass, without even a care,
Until one day they start, and sniff at the air.
All ears prick forward, eyes dart front and back,
Then all of a sudden, one breaks from the pack.
For just at that instant, their eyes have met;
Together again, both person and pet.
So they run to each other, these friends from long past,
The time of their parting is over at last.
The sadness they felt while they were apart,
Has turned into joy once more in each heart.
They embrace with a love that will last forever,
And then, side-by-side, they cross over... together.

MURPHY who lived in Norfolk, UK

My favourite pastime was to be with my Mum and Dad - they called me 'Their Velcro baby'

My beautiful boy Murphy was born in Belton, Norfolk, UK on the 11th September 2005. A date everyone will remember, he would have been 9 this year but sadly God had other plans for him. Murphy went to play over Rainbow Bridge on the 12th May this year and there isn't a day that goes by that I don't miss and cry for him.

We moved to Belton in 2012, Murphy's birth place. He had come home but sadly none of his family were still here. I did put an advert in our village news letter but sadly no joy. He made friends with two springers Lennie and Sylvie who are my friend Lesley's and they got on ok, had fun and became best friends. It was strange, two friends with springers and both called Lesley.

In our previous home there were so many fields and I really do believe that Murphy was at home there. He was in his element, every day we went out and he would race round the fields with his ears flapping, as though he was going to take off. He was the happiest springer ever.

The saddest thing is Murphy never went in water. How I wish I had seen him swim. On the beach he was the only dog with dry feet. That is the only thing I regret him never doing but he did so many other things that made me smile.

Murphy's favourite pastime was to be with us, he was a real Velcro baby and stuck to us like glue – where we went he was there. He was our shadow and we wouldn't have had him any other way; watching him lay his head on our feet or on the coffee table, we would say 'is your head too heavy, Murphy Dog?' then those big brown eyes would stare and look right into our souls, I miss the stares, I miss everything about him.

When Murphy came into our lives he was 12 weeks old, he had already been in another home, but not his forever home, we gave him that, all 8yrs 8 months and it was the best 8yrs 8 months of our lives. After our two girls had left home he was our fur baby boy. When he left us, he left a huge void in our lives. So empty and so quiet at home.

One day there might be a little fur baby that will help with our emptiness, but at the moment our hearts are still very broken and we miss our Murphy very much.

R.I.P. Our Beautiful Murphy Dog x

DODGE who lived in Trimly, Suffolk, UK

I used to love to pick up stones and put them in a row on the beach!

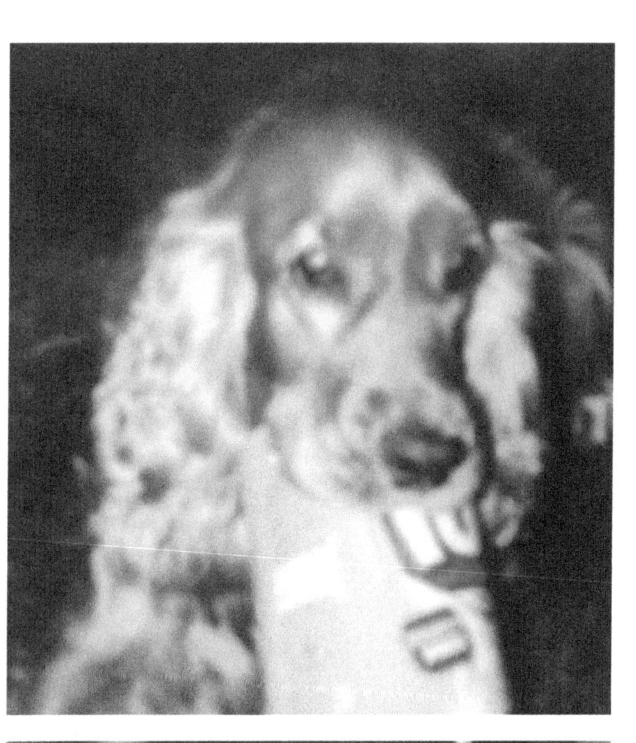

Name	Dodge
Birthdate	Unknown
My Mum	Annie
I live in	Trimly, Suffolk
My favourite toy	Teddy that looked just like me. Goes everywhere with me including rainbow bridge
I sleep	Mum and dad's bed
Favourite treat	anything tasty.
Other favourite treat	Dental stick
Good habits	Very good with children and when in a good mood, a good cuddler
Bad habits	biting mum when feeling grumpy.
Other bad habits	growling at people when they looked at me in the car.
Favourite walk	Meeting up with other cockers across the local field
Favourite activity	Pick up stones on the beach and putting them in a row on the beach.
My friends	Sam and cocker spaniel gang!

As soon as my mum and dad met me they wanted to take me home

We spent a long time getting to know this beautiful boy who was desperately needing a forever home. We were still heartbroken from losing Blue and had a huge hole in our hearts.

Eventually it was agreed that if he and Sam (our other dog) were ok together, we could take him. So it was up to Sam, we introduced them and after the usual doggy sniffing we took them for a nice walk together. On the way back they walked side by as if they had been together forever. Sam had got another companion, so all our hearts had been lifted.

On the way home Dodge climbed onto my lap and slept in my arms all the way home. Two dogs in the bedroom again that night.

Dodgy settled in very well, but as he did, we also became aware of another side to this little chap, glazed eyes and a curled lip happened from time to time for no real reason. Sam was not bothered about it as Blue had been the dominant one, so another grumpy little man didn't bother him, and there were no serious arguments. However, this is when we thought Dodgy was a better name than Bobby (which was his original name), they sounded alike and he responded to it straight away.

After about two weeks we had been out one evening, when we got home we gave both dogs a treat. Dodge curled his lip at me, glazed eyes and went to bite me. There was no reason for this as he had always been fine when I had given him treats, but he was not going to let us near him. He sat snarling at us, so we both sat on the floor talking quietly to him. After about 20 minutes it was as if someone had turned a switch, he got up wagging his tiny stumpy tail, came to us as if nothing had happened. These little incidents happened throughout the rest of his life, but I am convinced he didn't even realise it was happening. Our vets thought it was cocker rage syndrome, maybe this was why he had been up for rehoming or maybe dumped in the first place, one thing though, his forever home was going to be with us, we learnt to cope with these little upsets, with quiet talking and patience.

When we got Dodge he had a lovely silky coat, grooming wasn't a problem, but as he had been neutered his coat became woolly and his grooming became a real problem. Dodge became very grumpy when we wanted to brush his coat and so we had to find a groomer. Harriett (our recommended groomer) arrived in a van fully equipped with everything. I was really worried about how Dodge would react as I had had several nasty nips, so to be on the safe side I muzzled him. Harriett laughed at me and within 5 minutes the muzzle was off and she was working on him.

Harriette was a lovely lady. Loud, bubbly, always chatting and laughing. We became good friends but sadly she passed away a couple of years ago. I miss her; I don't know what we would have done without her. She would come every 6 weeks to clip, bath and clean teeth and ears. Dodge did try his luck a few times, but he would look over her shoulder at me, and glare, she would just laugh at him. He must have secretly enjoyed it as every time Harriett arrived he would scream with delight and run over to her!

When we had had Dodge about 5 years, our lovely Sam went to Rainbow Bridge, he was 10 years old. Dodge was now an only dog and to be honest he loved it. He came everywhere with us. We were always aware of his 'little

problem' as we called it and took precautions with people. I suffered several bites if his mood was not good, mainly when trying to remove burrs after his walks.

He had almost 7yrs with us and I'm sure they were the happiest of his life. We never knew how old he was, what his life had been like before us or where he came from.

As a tribute to Blue he came to us and we loved him dearly. We still miss him, after a very short and sudden illness, he went to rainbow bridge.

What a character our Dodgy was and so sadly missed. RIP

BLUE who lived in Trimly, Suffork, UK

I loved to steal flowerpots!

Name	Blue
Birthdate	10/09/96
My Mum	Annie
I live in	Trimly, Suffolk
My favourite toy	Kong stuffed with cheese
I sleep	Mum and dad's bed
Favourite treat	Cheese
Other favourite treat	going out in the car
Good habits	Loving and cuddly
Bad habits	tearing up toilet rolls
Other bad habits	stealing flower pots
Favourite walk	Trimly foreshore
Favourite activity	going on shoot with dad and retrieving birds.
My friends	Sam and Scruffy (little Jack Russell)!

Over twenty years ago I was working in a pet shop; regulars would bring their dogs in with them. One of these was a lovely black working cocker, she melted my heart, such a lovely girl, so when her owner told me they were going to let her have a litter before having her spayed, we decided to have one, even though we weren't planning on having another dog at that time. We were able to take first pick. How could we refuse!

We couldn't wait for the great day, when they were a few weeks old we went to see them. A chubby little blue roan boy picked us. He was our boy Blue, and at eight weeks old he came home to us, or I should say took over! At the time we had a dear old black lab Kestrel and a good tempered Jack Russell, Scruff. Their quiet life was shattered, but they both took to Blue in no time and by the end of the day they were all sleeping in Kestrel's bed. (Mind you Blue didn't spend the night there, he was in our bed.)

Blue turned into a great boy, mischievous, funny, a real cocker. I whistle trained him and he went on many shoots flushing and retrieving, a true working cocker. After a few years Blue lost his best pal Kestrel, but he and Scruff still got on well. They all had some really good times together over the years and we had really got the cocker bug.

One Sunday evening while my husband was grooming Blue he felt two small lumps in his neck. We took him to the vets the next day. Our vet seemed concerned and had Blue in for tests. The outcome was shattering to say the least; our gorgeous Blue had cancer. We were devastated; he was 7 years old, 8 weeks later he went to the rainbow bridge.

The other heartbreak was a few years before, our son had a domestic and came home with a son and a 4 month old pup called Sam. After a few days my son and child returned home, Sam stayed! Scruff had gone to rainbow bridge a few months before Blue at the age of 18yrs, now all we had was Sam. He had never been an only dog and we all grieved dreadfully over Blue. Sam was in a bad way, tearing about the house, opening doors, doing everything to look for Blue. We decided to look for a rescue in memory to Blue and as we had the cocker bug, we thought a cocker it had to be.

So after many calls to people in our dog circle, someone had a
red boy needing a forever home. Along came Dodge!!

BASIL who lived in Hastings, East Sussex, UK

I loved an apple every night at 7.00pm but before I ate it, I had to pull the stalk out first!

Name	Basil
Birthdate	06/05/2004 to 26/05/2014
My Mum	Paula
My Dad	Paul
I live in	St Leonards on Sea, near Hastings, East Sussex
My favourite toy	Ball
I sleep	with my mum and dad on their bed.
Favourite treat	Apples! I had one every night at 7 o'clock but I have to pull the stalk out first.
Other favourite treat	Popcorn. I was really good at catching popcorn when my brother & sisters threw it up in the air
Good habits	if I was dirty, I would jump in the bath as soon as I got in so mummy could give me a soapy shower & blow-dry. I let mummy hit the snooze button lots of times before I made her get up.
Bad habits	I liked to bark lots in the garden to get mummy to throw the ball for me.
Other bad habits	I liked yoghurt pots and then chewing them up & leaving bits all all over the floor
Favourite walk	Beach! I loved going swimming & on Christmas Day I always got a swim in the sea even though mum and dad said it was too cold
Favourite activity	going to the Country park to play fetch & lose expensive throwing toys
My friends	I lived with a boxer called Tia who came to live with us when we were both 5. My favourite friends are my human brother and sisters. My favourite human is my little sister Anni, because we were born in the same year & she liked to read me stories.

My name is Basil. I was the last of a litter of 8 and the breeders nick-named me "two brown patches"

I used to love sitting on my mum and dad's lap even though I might have been

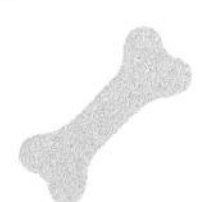

a bit too big. I didn't think I was, in my mind I was still the size of a puppy. You're never too big for a lap cuddle!

One of my favourite games was to catch popcorn when it was thrown up in the air. I used to get to play a great game and eat some lovely popcorn!

If mummy had minstrels or maltsters I would get a sneaky one, which I had to crunch very quietly so no-one knew.

I loved babies, mainly because they drop food over the side of the high chair and I can eat it all up!

I absolutely loved mud; I reckon I was a hippo in a previous life because I could have rolled around in it all day! The muddier the better because afterwards my mum would give me a lovely bath and blow dry.

We once lost our daughter Ellie in town, we let Basil off the lead & he knew straight away that something was wrong - he was trained to "find" each one of us by name so I told him to "find Ellie"; straight away the springer in him took over - nose to the floor he found her within a couple of minutes!

I loved sitting on the patio in the rain just watching stuff. I would see all sorts of things.

My favourite holiday with my family was camping, I loved it.

If a child or adult walked passed & said "what a pretty dog" I would sit down & wait for them to stroke me. I loved nothing better than a belly rub in the middle of the street!

Lightning Source UK Ltd.
Milton Keynes UK
UKOW07f1225200915

258928UK00009B/35/P